HOME BREWING
FOR AMERICANS

HOME BREWING FOR AMERICANS

Mastering the art of brewing American and European type beers at home

by
DAVID G. MILLER

Amateur Winemaker Publications Ltd.,
South Street, Andover, Hants, U.K.

© Amateur Winemaker Publications Ltd.

Printed in Great Britain by:
Standard Press (Andover) Ltd., South Street, Andover, Hants.

1st Impression: 1981

ISBN 0 900841 61 3

TABLE OF CONTENTS

	page
Chapter 1 – Introduction	7
Chapter 2 – Commercial and Amateur Brewing Processes	9
I. Malting	9
II. Making Sweet Wort	9
III. Making Bitter Wort	10
IV. Fermentation	10
V. Bottling and Aging	11
Home Brewing	11
Chapter 3 – Basic Equipment for Home Brewing	13
Chapter 4 – Brewing Ingredients	19
I. Malt	19
II. Colored Malts	20
III. Adjuncts	21
IV. Malt Extracts	22
V. Sugar	22
VI. Water	23
VII. Hops	23
Buying and storing hops	25
Hop rates	26
Finishing hops and dry hopping	26
VIII. Yeast	27
IX. Additives	28
Chapter 5 – Extract Beers	31
Extract Light Ale	31
Extract Diet Lager	33
Adapting Grain Beer Recipes	34
Chapter 6 – Equipment for Grain Beer Brewing	35

Chapter 7 – Making Sweet Wort from Grain Malt . . . 39
   I. Grinding the Malt 39
  II. Water Treatment 39
        Water Analysis 40
 III. Cooking Cereal Adjuncts 44
 IV. Mashing 46
  V. Sparging 50
        Set Mash 54

Chapter 8 – Making Bitter Wort (Boiling) 55
        Hydrometer Reading 57
        Degrees of Extract 58

Chapter 9 – Fermentation 59
        Alcohol Content 61

Chapter 10 – Bottling, Aging and Serving 63
        Primary 63
        Aging 66
        Serving 67

Chapter 11 – Lager Beers 69
   I. Light Lagers 69
        Dutch Lager 70
        Scandinavian Lager 71
        American Lager 73
  II. Pale Lagers 74
        Pilsner-Style Lager 74
        Dortmund-Style Lager 75
 III. Dark Lagers 76
        American Bock 76
        Muenchner-Style Lager 77
        Einbeck-Style Lager 78

Chapter 12 – Ales 81
   I. Pale Ale 82
  II. Bitter 83
 III. Brown Ale 84
 IV. Stout and Porter 86

Chapter 13 – Problems 89
    I. Infections 89
    II. Haze 89
    III. Taste 90
    IV. Procedure 93
    V. Imaginary Problems 93

Chapter 14 – The Brewer's Calendar 95

Appendix A – An Outline of Home Brewing 99

Appendix B – Bibliography 100

Appendix C – Mail Order Sources 101

Appendix D – Equivalent Weights and Measures . . . 103

Glossary 104

Index 108

Chapter 1

INTRODUCTION

Home brewing is a fascinating and rewarding hobby. If you enjoy mastering a craft and making something of your own, the way you want it, you will probably enjoy this pastime immensely.

In the past few years, a large number of people have felt the attraction of this ancient art and have tried it. Unfortunately, many have been discouraged by their results, and after searching for ways to improve their home brew, have given up in despair. The promise of home brewed Pilsner or Dortmunder was simply not kept by the stuff actually turned out in their basement breweries.

I can well understand this discouragement, because I have felt it myself. Fortunately, I was able to make a study of professional brewing methods and to discover what I was doing wrong. First, I discovered that the recipes I had been using called for very high hop rates and incorrect water treatment; then I learned that first class beer cannot be made from malt syrup. Professionals start with grain malt, and if you want to rival their results, so must you.

Let me hasten to add that there is no reason to be afraid of "mashing". Many accounts of this process are needlessly confusing and complex. Small-scale home brewers do not need to imitate slavishly the elaborate procedures of the commercial beer makers. And while you do need to understand the process to some degree, it is well within the grasp of amateurs. Let me also assure you that the extra time and effort you put into a grain beer are amply repaid by the results.

The purpose of this book is to present a simple, workable method of brewing all kinds of beers from American malt, using equipment and ingredients available in this country. Most of the information comes from my own trials and experiments. I have written this book so that you will not have to learn everything the hard way, as I did.

I have tried to explain all procedures so that a beginner can use them to brew a good beer on his first try. Experienced brewers should feel free to skip explanation of equipment with which they are already familiar. However, before attempting to mash, you should read the entire chapter. You may not have time to read each section as it comes up.

In the recipe section, I have emphasised lager beer, because that is the favorite brew of my countrymen. However, you will not find many recipes for American light lagers, first, because they are so much alike, and second, because making American-style beer is not much of a "paying proposition". The return on your labor is far greater if you brew European-style beers. (As of writing this, imported lager is selling for twenty dollars a case.) I would also hope to tempt you to try your hand at some of the marvelous ales of Great Britain. Home brewing, like gourmet cooking, is an international adventure. Now – let's get started!

Chapter 2

COMMERCIAL AND AMATEUR BREWING

Beer is made from grain, water, hops, and yeast. The basic process is the same in amateur and commercial breweries. The five steps are:

I. MALTING

In this first stage, whole grain – usually barley – is soaked in water and then allowed to sprout. Rootlets begin to appear at one end of the grain, and the embryonic barley plant, called the *acrospire*, begins to grow inside. When the acrospire reaches a predetermined length, the growth is stopped by drying the so-called "green malt" in a large oven, or *kiln*. At first, the kiln temperature is kept low; later, as water is driven out, the temperature may be raised somewhat.

Both the degree of growth of the acrospire and the final kilning temperature have a profound effect on the type of malt produced. As the acrospire grows, catalysts known as *enzymes* are produced and modify the contents of the grain. Thus, the degree of growth is called by the maltster the degree of *modification*. Modification involves both starches and proteins: as the acrospire grows, the enzymes reduce both to simpler (smaller molecular) forms. Barley starch is modified to malt starch, and barley proteins are broken down into simpler malt proteins.

The temperature of kilning determines the color of the malt husk and, therefore, of the beer made from it. British pale malt is more modified and more roasted than American or Continental lager malt; this explains why British "pale ale" is darker than pale lager.

II. MAKING SWEET WORT

Malt is mostly starch, which is not useful for brewing beer. The malt starch must be converted into fermentable sugars by enzymes produced during malting. This starch conversion results in the sugary liquid known as sweet wort.

The first step in making sweet wort is to grind the malt, which exposes the powdery interiors. The grain is then mixed with hot water, which releases and activates the malt enzymes. This steeping process is known as *mashing*. British malt is mashed in a single-temperature process at about 152 degrees Fahrenheit. Elsewhere, the grain is mashed at a lower temperature (95–122°F) first, to permit protein conversion. (Lager malt is much richer in protein than ale malt.) After the "protein rest" the temperature is boosted to 152°F for starch conversion.

Lager malt is rich in *diastase* (starch-converting enzymes) and often unmalted grain – usually corn or rice – is cooked and added to the mash, where its starch is converted along with the malt starch. Thus these unmalted cereals, or *adjuncts*, permit the brewer to get more sugar from a given amount of malt.

When starch conversion is complete, the resulting sugary porridge is drained in a large vessel called a *lauter tub* with a false bottom full of holes. When as much liquid as possible has drained off, the grains are rinsed, or *sparged*, with hot water to wash out the remaining sugar. This completes the production of sweet wort.

III. MAKING BITTER WORT

Bitter wort is made by boiling the sweet wort with *hops* for one to two hours. The hop plant is a long, spindly vine; only the flowers, or cones, of the female plant are used in brewing. These cones contain various resins and aromatic oils which give beer its characteristic bitterness. Boiling extracts and dissolves these flavoring substances in the wort. The type and amount of hops used profoundly affect the flavor of the finished beer.

IV. FERMENTATION

After boiling, the bitter wort is transferred to a large vat for cooling. When cool, it is mixed, or *pitched*, with a pure strain of brewer's yeast. Yeast is a low form of plant life which has the ability to convert sugar into approximately equal quantities of carbon dioxide gas and alcohol. This process is known as *fermentation*. The *primary* stage of fermentation takes two to seven days; after this rapid fermentation, a slower stage, called *secondary* fermentation, begins. This takes anywhere from four to fourteen days to complete, depending on temperature and other factors.

V. BOTTLING AND AGING

When secondary fermentation is over, some beers (such as ales) are artificially or naturally carbonated, then bottled or casked. Aging takes place in the bottle.

Lager beers, on the other hand, are transferred to large tanks and aged at cool temperatures (32–40°F) for one to six months. This long, cold aging is known as *lagering* (from the German verb meaning "to store"). It is then carbonated and bottled or casked, and is ready to drink.

HOME BREWING

Amateurs follow the same sequence of steps as commercial brewers, with only a few differences. The most significant is that most amateurs begin with the third step by using malt extract, which is simply concentrated sweet wort. Dedicated amateurs begin with the second step, grinding and mashing grain malt to make their own sweet wort. It is virtually impossible for the average urban hobbyist to malt his own barley, and he could not do as good a job as the commercial maltsters in any case. However, this is not the case with sweet wort.

Malt extract syrups and powders are inferior to freshly made sweet wort and give a distinct "off taste" to the finished beer. This taste is particularly noticeable in pale, delicately hopped lagers. I consider it worthwhile to begin home brewing with a batch or two of extract beer in order to gain experience with boiling, fermentation and bottling. But most people soon become dissatisfied with the extract flavor. Because of this fact, and because there are already many books in print on the subject of extract beers, this one is mostly concerned with making beer from grain. However, extract beers are dealt with as a preliminary step in learning the craft of home brewing.

The other difference between amateur and commercial brewing

is in the last step. All homemade beers, including lagers, are aged in the bottle. This makes no difference in the finished product. Lager is commercially aged in vats because that is the most efficient way to do it on a large scale. At home, the low cost of beer bottles and the requirements of natural carbonation make bottle aging more practical.

Now that you understand what you will be doing, it is time to get ready to do it, by getting together the equipment and ingredients that you will need.

Chapter 3

BASIC EQUIPMENT FOR HOME BREWING

In this chapter I will cover those items of equipment which are essential for making any kind of beer at home. For brewing grain beers, a few other items are needed; they are discussed in Chapter Six.

Boiler. Since home brewing includes boiling the wort with hops, a large boiling vessel with a lid is needed. This should have a capacity of at least five gallons; seven or eight is better. Suitable materials are stainless steel, copper, and enamelware. The cheapest alternative is a 5¼ gallon (21 quart) enamelware canner. I use an 8¼ gallon model which is slightly more expensive. Try to find one of these canners at a discount store during canning season; it will probably cost more at other times of the year.

Primary Fermenter. Home brewers use ten-gallon plastic trash cans for their five-gallon brews. Do not be tempted by the incredibly low prices of some of the cheaper brands. These are made from inferior plastic which will get brittle and crack after a few exposures to boiling hot bitter wort. Get a good, heavy-duty brand such as Rubbermaid, preferably with handles and a close-fitting lid. Plastic sheeting can be used to cover an open primary, but an ordinary lid is much easier to clean.

Secondary Fermenter. Homemade beer must be siphoned, or *racked*, into a closed container for the second phase of fermentation. The usual choices are a semirigid plastic cube or a glass carboy, both of five gallon capacity. Many winemakers' stores carry both of these; if you prefer glass, carboys are usually a bit cheaper from a bottled water company.

Airlock. To keep air away from the beer during secondary fermentation, a one-way valve called an airlock is attached to the mouth of the carboy. It lets carbon dioxide gas escape without letting air in. Rubber stoppers and airlocks are sold at all winemakers' stores.

Racking Tube, Hose and Bottle Filler. These are used for racking and bottling. You need about six feet of clear plastic hose. The racking tube is a rigid plastic tube with an inlet about one inch from the bottom; this enables you to siphon beer out of the primary and leave the dregs behind. The bottle filler is a rigid plastic tube with a spring-loaded valve in the bottom, which enables you to fill each bottle in turn without pinching the hose or spilling beer while moving from bottle to bottle. Again, these items are available at all winemakers' stores.

Bottles and Capper. Five gallons of beer equal about 53 bottles. Returnable beer bottles, bought from friends or liquor stores for the price of the deposit, are the most usual choice. Imported beer bottles taking a regular crown cap are also satisfactory, as are champagne bottles. "Twist-or-pry" threaded-mouth throwaway bottles are *not*. A home brewer usually needs about thirty gallons' worth of beer bottles once he gets his operation going.

Bottle cappers and caps are available in various styles and prices from hardware stores, as well as winemakers' shops. Expensive cappers are generally easier to use, but they all work.

Cleaning Supplies. If you do not own a dishwasher, consider a bottle washer that uses water pressure. These are available at winemakers' stores. Also, a piece of rag or sponge stapled to a dowel rod will probably be necessary. Bottle brushes do not work as well as a homemade cleaner. Sponges and a nylon scouring pad are available at supermarkets. Special chlorine detergent, available at winemakers' stores, should be used to sterilize everything that touches your beer.

Scale. A postage scale, weighing up to eight ounces in quarter-ounce increments, is needed for weighing out hops. Guesswork will not do, because many hop packages vary markedly from their stated weights. Office supply stores are the best source for scales.

For brewing grain beers, an ordinary ten-pound household scale is helpful.

Hydrometer and Jar. The hydrometer is a small glass instrument for measuring the *specific gravity* of wort and beer. I have already explained that wort is a solution of water and malt sugar. Any volume – say, a quart – of sugar solution will weigh more than the same volume of pure water. The more sugar there is in the solution, the heavier it will be. Specific gravity is a measure of this excess weight. If you float a hydrometer in a sample of wort and it reads 1.050, this means that the five gallons of wort will weigh 1.05 times the same volume of water. Now, after the wort is pitched with yeast and begins to ferment, the yeast consumes the sugar and converts it into carbon dioxide (which escapes) and alcohol (which is lighter than water).

Basic Brewing Equipment. Front row: *Bottle capper, hydrometer and test jar, bottles, eight gallon boiler.* Back row: *thermometer, plastic colander, carboy (secondary fermenter) with airlock, and plastic trash can (primary fermenter). Leaning against the primary are the racking tube and clear plastic hose,* left, *and bottle filler,* right.

Thus, as fermentation goes on, the specific gravity of the fermenting beer will slowly drop. A typical beer with a starting specific gravity of 1.050 (usually shortened to just "fifty") will ferment out to a terminal specific gravity of about 1.012 (or twelve). Thus, by taking specific gravity readings, you can keep track of the fermentation of your beer and determine when it is finished fermenting. When fermentation ceases, the specific gravity will no longer drop.

Be sure to buy a hydrometer with a specific gravity scale. Some hydrometers are designed only for winemakers and will have other scales; many have both winemakers' and specific gravity scales. If you get one of these, be *sure* to use the S.G. scale for brewing.

The test jar is a small cylinder for holding the wort sample while you are taking readings. It is usually sold in a set with the hydrometer, but be sure to get one in any case. You will also need an ordinary rubber-bulb kitchen baster for drawing wort samples out of the closed secondary fermenter.

Thermometer. This is also used to keep track of fermentation. A dairy or cheese thermometer, with a range from 32° to 212°F will do for all brewing purposes, including mashing. Good thermometers are available at winemakers' and gourmet cooking stores.

Spoon. A large wooden spoon is best for stirring; stainless steel will do, but may chip the enamel on your boiler. Do not use your wooden spoon to stir spaghetti sauce, or you will end up with a plate of hop flavored spaghetti and five gallons of garlicky lager!

Pots and Pans. A two-quart saucepan, and a two-quart teakettle, are already on hand in most kitchens, as are measuring spoons and cups and a Pyrex measuring pitcher of one quart capacity.

Strainer. You need a big one. My first choice is a large plastic colander lined with eight layers of cheesecloth, or four layers of fine-mesh mosquito netting. A few spring clothespins will hold your "filter element" in place while you pour the hot bitter wort from the boiler into the primary.

Jugs. A one-gallon and half-gallon glass jug are both useful. The half-gallon size is perfect for making a starter (see the chapter on Fermenting); the one-gallon will hold extra brewing water and can be used to mark one-gallon levels on the outside of your primary fermenter. Just pour in one gallon, mark the level, and repeat until you reach the nine-gallon mark. This procedure, of course, need only be done once, and is well worth the trouble.

Notebook. An ordinary spiral notebook and a pen are two of the brewer's most important tools. Write down everything you do, every time you brew. Do not trust your memory – it will cost you in time, money and bad beer if you do. Instead, take systematic notes: write down the recipe and brewing procedure (including all times and temperatures) when you start a batch. Then, make further *dated* entries to record hydrometer readings, temperatures, appearance, treatment given, racking and bottling – any and every fact about your brewing. A well-kept log will help you learn from your mistakes, rather than merely suffer from them.

Chapter 4

BREWING INGREDIENTS

I. MALT

All American malt not otherwise labeled is pale lager malt. It is high in proteins, but rich in diastase. It must be mashed by a two-temperature process, including a "protein rest" as well as a "sugar rest", but the entire process only requires about an hour and a half because of the abundance of enzymes.

Good pale lager malt will contain very little straw or other debris. The grains will be of uniform size and will crush easily.

Basic brewing ingredients. Front row, from left: *shredded hops, loose hops, envelope and foil packet of yeast.* Middle row: *Rice, pale lager malt, dark crystal malt, roast barley (unmalted equivalent of chocolate malt).* Back row: *Corn grits, pearl barley, malt extract, and corn sugar.*

Not all grades of malt are suitable for brewing. Inferior malt is used to make breakfast cereals and whiskey, among other things. Therefore I recommend buying malt only from a reputable winemakers' store.

II. COLORED MALTS

These are used in small amounts to add color and flavor to darker beers.

Crystal Malt is made as follows: when the acrospire reaches the proper length, the moist grain is *not* slowly dried; instead, the temperature is boosted to "mash heat" (150°F) and starch conversion takes place *in the grain itself*. The malt is then kilned.

When you break open a grain of crystal malt, you will find that it contains not malt flour, but a golden or reddish-golden lump of malt sugar. Since crystal malt is already converted, it does not need mashing. However, it is usually added to the mash kettle in making grain beers, since its acidity promotes starch conversion. For extract beers, it is simply crushed and boiled with the bitter wort.

Crystal malt is available in two types, roasted to a greater or lesser degree. The degree of roasting affects the flavor as well as color. Most unlabeled crystal malt is what I call "dark", with a brownish-red interior. If your recipe calls for pale crystal malt, you can substitute one ounce of dark for two ounces of pale. However, the flavor will not be exactly the same. I prefer pale crystal malt for pale lagers, and dark crystal for dark lagers and all ales.

Chocolate Malt is ordinary pale malt, roasted to a brown color. It gives a smooth, mellow "roasted" flavor to dark beers. For extract beers, it is crushed and boiled in the wort; while for grain beers, it is crushed and mashed, just like pale malt or crystal malt.

Black Patent Malt is similar to chocolate malt, but roasted dead black, with a sharper, more acid flavor. Use sparingly – three ounces will turn five gallons of pale beer deep brown.

Roast Barley. Roast barley is simply unmalted barley which has been roasted dark brown in a kiln. In color it is between chocolate malt and black patent malt. Its flavor, however, is different from either, and it gives a delicious dry smoothness to dark ales and stouts. It is first choice for Porter and Stout (recipes on pages 86 and 87). It can be crushed and boiled in an extract wort, or mashed in the kettle with pale malt.

III. ADJUNCTS

Adjuncts are unmalted cereals used to "stretch" malt. Their main effect is to produce a paler, lighter bodied, less "malty" beer. (The exception is barley, which is used mainly in stout and ale.) In Germany, the use of adjuncts is outlawed in order to preserve the traditional full body and flavor of German lager. However, American and Dutch lagers require adjuncts in order to get the very light color and flavor which are characteristic for them.

Some adjuncts can be bought as *flakes*, pre-cooked and ready to add to the mash kettle. In this form they are quite expensive, but very convenient for amateurs to use. The common adjuncts are:

Rice. This adjunct is almost pure starch and has very little flavor of its own. It is used in Dutch and some American lagers, and in British pale ale. The only usable form available in this country is the uncooked, polished grains. Short or medium grain is cheaper; instant or converted rices are very costly and not suitable. Rice must be thoroughly washed and boiled before mashing.

Corn. This adjunct has a sweet taste that can be detected in Scandinavian and most American beers. Some American breweries use 40% corn in their mashes. Corn can be bought as flakes, but I would not recommend Kellogg's for your beer: too many additives and preservatives, including table salt and cane sugar. Special brewing cornflakes, available from some winemakers' stores, are better. Low-sodium cornflakes sold by health food stores are also satisfactory. Corn can also be bought as "grits" in the cooked cereals section of most supermarkets. They must be washed and boiled like rice before mashing.

Barley. Unmalted barley has a smooth, grainy flavor, and its high protein content makes for a good head. Unfortunately, it also makes for hazy beer, and so is best reserved for stout and very dark ales. Barley flakes are available from winemakers' stores; alternatively, pearl barley from the supermarket can be washed and cooked like rice.

IV. MALT EXTRACTS

As explained above, malt extracts are simply concentrated worts in either syrup or dry powder form. I have tried a number of brands and have yet to find one that does not have a distinct "extract" tang to it. Perhaps the manufacturing process of removing all or most of the water from the wort in a low-temperature vacuum evaporator somehow alters the chemical makeup of the wort.

In any case, malt extracts are available in dark and light versions, hopped and unhopped, at a variety of prices. Grocery store brands are inferior, but so are some much more expensive types sold in winemakers' stores. Unhopped extracts are preferable, because using your own fresh hops gives a superior brew. It is also better to use light extract for dark beers, and add crushed dark malts to the boiler to get the best "roast malt" flavor.

V. SUGAR

British recipes call for various forms of cane sugar. However, I must say that, especially for pale beers, I agree with the standard American position that corn sugar (dextrose) gives a better flavor. Cane sugar seems to leave a sour taste in the finished beer.

Let me add that I also believe sugar must be used with caution in any case. The more sugar you put in your beer, the drier and thinner (less full-bodied) it will be. Sugar ferments completely into alcohol and carbon dioxide, leaving no residue of complex, unfermentable sugars to sweeten the beer and give it its characteristic malty taste. Thus the use of sugar seems to me contrary to the whole idea of grain beer brewing. Even in Britain the use of sugar is, by historical standards, a recent development, often lamented by lovers of "real ale". Lagers, even the lightest of them, are brewed from grain only. (The sole exception to this rule is the new breed of "diet beers", which in the author's opinion do not deserve to be called beer at all.)

VI. WATER

Almost any safe drinking water can be used to make extract beer. Water *does* affect flavor, however, and for grain beers, alkaline water can cause problems with mashing. See Chapter Seven for an explanation of water treatment for mashing, and a list of supplies needed.

VII. HOPS

Hops are one of the most important and expensive ingredients in beer. The bitter resins humulon and lupulon (alpha and beta acid) are powerful preservatives, and hops were originally used in beer to improve its keeping qualities. It was soon recognized, however, that the hops' bitterness was a perfect match for the sweetness of malt.

Many winemakers' stores carry a variety of hops. Most of these are grown domestically, but some imported types are available. The most common types are these:

Cluster. This is *the* American hop, used in almost all standard domestic beers. It is pungent and, like many American strains, it can impart a harsh aftertaste if too much is used. This characteristic helps to explain the low hop rates of American beers.

Cascade. This American strain has a beautiful, flowery, yet stinging aroma. It is my first choice for light lagers. However, it works best in hard water, where the gypsum seems to "soften" its bitterness, and in moderate amounts – not more than one ounce per five gallons.

Bullion. This is an English breed, but originally from American stock, and even today it is rejected by conservative British brewmasters because of its "American" flavor! It is a very bitter hop, which makes it economical to use; however, its strong, distinctive taste means that it should not be used "straight". For dark ales and stouts, up to one ounce per five gallons can be used.

Brewer's Gold. Another English breed from American stock; its flavor and aroma are much more "British" and it is therefore a good choice for ales and stout.

Northern Brewer. This is yet another English-American breed, but even in Britain it is accepted as having a true British flavor. It is also grown seedless on the Continent and used in lagers brewed there.

Fuggles. This is a native British strain, spicy, mild, and low in bitterness. It is grown seedless in America and only the domestic version is sold here. British hops are hard to ship owing to the method of storage used in England.

Golding. This is considered the finest English hop for flavor and aroma, and is first choice for all the lighter colored ales. It has somewhat more bittering power than Fuggles. Again, only the home-grown seedless version is available here.

Hallertau. A mellow, spicy hop with a beautiful aroma and flavor, perfect for dark lagers and for light lagers as well. The aroma is not as pungent as Cascade or Saaz. It is grown north of Munich, and real Muenchner beer requires Hallertau hops. Both imported and home-grown versions are sometimes available.

Tettnanger. This is another fine German hop, generally similar to Hallertau and suitable for all types of lagers. I have seen only the home-grown variety for sale in the U.S.A.

Saaz. The most famous pale lager in the world is Pilsner, and the most sought-after hop for pale lagers is the Saaz (pronounced "zotz"). This hop is grown in Bohemia (western Czechoslovakia) near Pilsen, and is used exclusively in brewing the only true Pilsner beer, Pilsner Urquell. It has a sharp, dusky flavor and pungent aroma which make it a perfect match for a pale, high-gravity, all-malt wort. This hop should not be wasted in extract beers. It is available only in the original, imported version, is one of the most expensive hops on the market; and is worth every penny you pay for it.

Buying and Storing Hops

If you have the space, you should store all your hops in plastic bags in the refrigerator freezing compartment or deep freeze. After you find your own favorites, you can buy a pound or two at a time and insure yourself against temporary shortages. Hops are a seasonal crop and are thus not always available, and dealers do run out. However, you must freeze hops for long storage. For shorter term storage – up to three months – the refrigerator will serve. Remember with any type of hops to date the packages and try to use the oldest first.

Hops are available in four different forms. Whole, loose-packed cones are sold in one- to eight-ounce bags, sometimes labeled "finishing hops". The loose pack makes it easy to spot mold and other defects, but loose hops are of all forms the most vulnerable to spoilage. A reputable dealer will store his loose hops in the refrigerator, and will not mind selling you a cold package rather than the one on the shelf.

Compressed hops are sold in blocks, usually of four ounces. In this form it is hard to judge their condition, but with a little experience your nose will tell you if they smell fresh or stale. Compressed hops should always be wrapped in plastic and preferably stored in the refrigerator.

Imported hops are usually shredded, then compressed into large blocks and sealed under nitrogen. This is virtually as good as freezing. After shipment, the dealer breaks up the blocks and re-packages them in four-ounce plastic bags. Once broken down, these hops are vulnerable and should be refrigerated or frozen.

The most modern form of hops is the pelletized. Looking at them in the bag, you might mistake them for rabbit food. The hops are powdered and then pressed into small pellets. Sealed under nitrogen, they are almost immune to spoilage, but in an ordinary plastic bag, they still need refrigeration or freezing.

One reason you need a hop scale is that it is virtually impossible to "guesstimate" an eight-ounce bag of hops into one-ounce or smaller units. An error of even a quarter of an ounce will make a noticeable difference in the bitterness of the beer. Another problem is that hop packages are not reliable. A one-ounce bag of "finishing" hops may weigh as much as one and a quarter ounces, and the weights stated on other types of packages are likewise minimums rather than guarantees. No one should mind getting more than he paid for in a bag of hops, but in the finished beer, the result may be more bitterness than he wants!

Hop Rates

All hops grown in North America and Continental Europe – that is to say, all hops sold in the United States – are seedless. Seedless hops have a much higher bittering power per ounce (alpha acid content) than seeded, British hops of the same variety. This difference largely accounts for the lower hop rates quoted in my ale recipes, as compared with those found in British books.

Besides the actual figures, another problem with most amateur recipes is that they go by ounces, without specifying the type of hops to be used. Many beers can only be made from one or two hop types (Muenchner, for example), and even where there is a choice, you cannot simply substitute blindly. Hops vary in their bittering power as well as flavor, and you need to take this fact into account. My original draft of this chapter included an explanation of Dave Line's Alpha Acid Unit system for estimating bitterness. Unfortunately, in America the alpha acid content of hops sold to amateurs is almost never stated; thus Americans cannot use this excellent system. The best you can do is to follow the recipes exactly as given and then adjust them if the first batch is too bitter – or not bitter enough – for your taste. If you must substitute hop types, make a guess as to relative bitterness and try to go from there. Remember, Americans are used to very lightly-hopped beers, so if you must guess, guess low in setting hop rates.

Finishing Hops and Dry Hopping

Bitterness is determined by the amount and type of hops that are boiled with the wort. However, during a one-hour boil, many volatile aromatic oils are driven off or destroyed. To give more hop flavor and aroma, a small quantity of hops is stirred in at the end of the boil. These are called finishing hops, and should be as fresh as possible. They are left to soak in the hot bitter wort for about an hour before straining off. For even more aroma, a second quantity of hops, called dry hops, is added to the beer during secondary fermentation. Not all beers need both these treatments; in general, the paler the beer, the more it will benefit from them.

Finishing hops need not be loose cones, and not all loose hops are fresh. Choose a good variety, but don't worry about the type of package the hops came in. Let your nose be your guide.

VIII. YEAST

There are two distinct types of beer yeast: lager yeast (*Saccharomyces Carlsbergensis*) and ale yeast (*Saccharomyces cerevisiae*). They are sometimes called bottom- and top-fermenting, though in small volume fermentations the rapid working of ale yeast is more apparent than its supposed top fermentation. Both types will settle out when fermentation is over.

The yeasts differ in two important respects. First there is the working temperature: Lager yeast works from about 40° to 60°F, ideally, though it can be used at higher temperatures. Ale yeast works from about 55° to 70°F ideally. This difference in working temperature is reflected in the more rapid fermentation of ale yeast. You should try to ferment your beer at the proper temperature for the yeast you are using. For ale, this means cool room temperatures; for lager, a cold basement.

The other important difference between the yeast types is their "attenuation" or ability to ferment sugars. Both will ferment maltose (simple malt sugar) but ale yeast, though it works faster than lager yeast, will not ferment dextrins (complex malt sugars) nearly as well as its slower cousin. In practice, this means that the same wort, fermented with ale yeast, will end up with much more dextrins than if it had been fermented with lager yeast. The result will be a sweeter beer, since the dextrins are responsible for sweetness. The difference in terminal specific gravity may be as much as six points with an all-malt wort.

You can see, then, that yeast types are *not* interchangeable and that a wort must be "designed" for the type of yeast it will be fermented with. My lager recipes are designed to give the proper degree of sweetness with lager yeast, while my ale recipes are likewise designed for ale yeast. If you are making a grain beer and *must* substitute one type of yeast for the other, study the recipes carefully and adjust your mash times to resemble those of the respective beer types. In practice, this would mean that a lager recipe to be fermented with ale yeast would require boost and starch conversion steps about twice as long as for lager yeast. Likewise, if you want to ferment an ale with lager yeast, cut the boost and starch conversion times approximately in half.

The only form of yeast available to amateurs is the freeze-dried granules. They usually come with instructions for activating in warm water, but I prefer to make a starter (see Chapter Nine). Observe the temperature recommendations carefully: excessive heat will kill the yeast and leave your beer open to infection.

I do not recommend trying to save yeast from one brew to the next. Commercial breweries do this routinely, but for an amateur, using a fresh yeast for every brew is very cheap insurance against the yeast going "off" or changing genetically during the fermentation. Compared to the total cost of your ingredients for a five gallon batch of beer – not to mention the time you spend making it – the savings are minuscule.

IX. ADDITIVES

Included in this category are many ingredients which are not strictly necessary for brewing, but helpful in getting good results.

Yeast Energizer. This is a vitamin and mineral supplement for beer yeast. It is helpful with beers made from malt extract; it is not needed with grain beers, though a pinch in the starter jug will speed up the activity of lager yeast.

Irish Moss. Actually a form of seaweed, this stuff is added during the boil and helps produce haze-free beers. Like yeast energizer, it is sold by winemakers' stores.

Gelatine. This is used to "clear" the beer of yeast after fermentation. Ordinary food grade gelatine is just about as effective as the special "finings" gelatine sold in winemakers' stores.

Vitamin C and Anti-oxidant. Both of these are used to prevent browning, hazes and off flavors due to contact with air; the former will give you an excuse to treat your cold with large doses of beer.

Either is added at racking or bottling time, and both are sold at winemakers' stores.

Campden Tablets (potassium metabisulfite). This is another preservative which, besides preventing oxidation, also inhibits the growth of wild yeasts and bacteria which can infect your beer. It is sold by all winemakers' stores.

Polyclar. This is an insoluble plastic polymer, sold in finely powdered form. It helps to prevent chill haze and removes oxidative browning. While its use is optional, I strongly recommend it. See Chapter Nine for an explanation of how to use it. Polyclar is sold by some winemakers' stores.

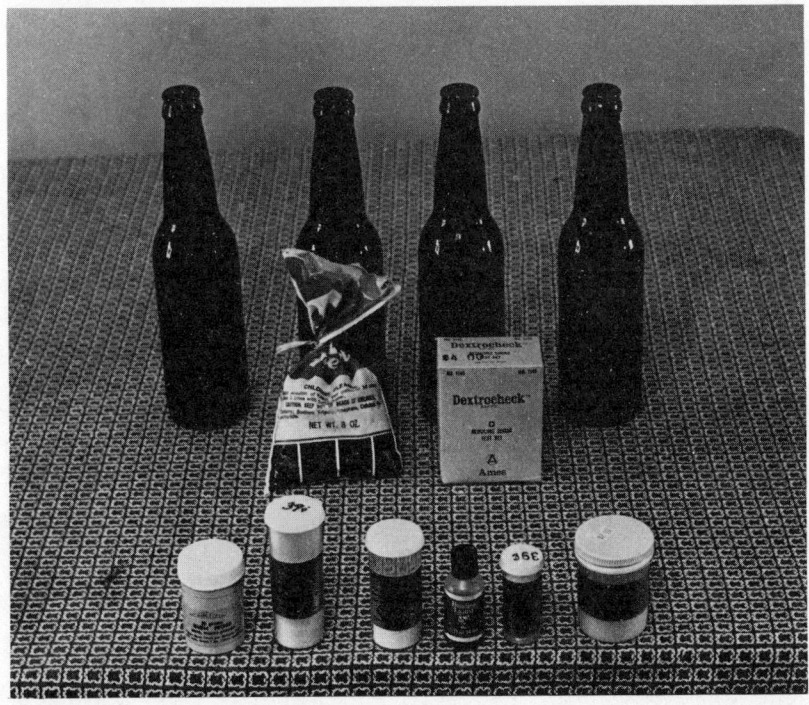

Additives and other useful items: front, from left, *Irish moss, finings, gelatine, Vitamin C, heading compound, Campden tablets, yeast energizer.* In the rear, *chlorine detergent* and the *Dextrocheck kit,* a convenient method of assuring nervous beginners that fermentation is really complete.

Heading Compounds. These are various organic substances which assure a firm, long-lasting head on a glass of beer. Full-bodied, mature grain beers rarely need heading assistance, but with a new recipe they are good insurance. I bottle and cap a few test bottles before adding heading compound to the rest of the batch; then, after aging, I can compare the heading properties of treated and untreated beer and decide whether to make the compound a permanent part of the recipe.

Heading compound should be used with caution. It is better to use too little than too much: even a headless beer is better than a glass full of undrinkable foam.

Gypsum. This is a soluble form of calcium sulfate. It is used to "harden" soft waters for brewing pale beers. Available at all winemakers' stores.

Chapter 5

EXTRACT BEERS

The making of sweet wort from malt extract is not very different from making orange juice from frozen concentrate. For a five gallon batch, the procedure is as follows:

1) Draw about a gallon of hot water from your kitchen tap into your boiler. Stir in the malt syrup or powder. If you are using syrup refill the container three times or more with hot water in order to rinse all the extract out. Rinse the lid as well.
2) Stir the mixture until you are certain that the extract is completely dissolved. Then add the corn sugar and gypsum (if called for) and stir again. Finally, fill the boiler with hot tap water up to a maximum of six gallons total volume. At least one gallon will be boiled off. If your boiler will not hold six gallons, fill it to a level about two inches from the rim.

The rest of the procedure for making extract beers is identical with that for grain beers. You should add a pinch of yeast energizer to your starter, and about half a teaspoon at racking time. Other than that, you are ready to skip to Chapter Eight after deciding on a recipe.

EXTRACT LIGHT ALE

I recommend trying something other than light lager for your first brew. Ale ferments and matures quickly, and most beginners are in a hurry. Also, no matter what recipe you try, it is not going to come out tasting like Budweiser (or whatever your favorite American beer is), so you will probably be happier if you know you are making ale, and it is not supposed to taste like "regular" beer. You will find, though, that it tastes very good!

Ingredients

    2½–3½ lbs. British Light malt extract
    2½–1½ lbs. corn sugar (to make a total of 5 lb. extract plus sugar)
    1 teaspoon gypsum
    1 oz. Brewer's Gold or Northern Brewer or 1½ oz. Fuggles hops (boil)
    ¼ oz. same type hops (finishing)
    ¼ oz. same type hops (dry hops – optional)
    1 teaspoon Irish Moss (optional)
    1 packet ale yeast
    1 teaspoon gelatine finings
    1 teaspoon Ascorbic Acid
    1¼ cups corn sugar (priming)
    Yeast energizer

Method

1. In the boiler, dissolve the extract and gypsum in 1 gallon hot tap water; add water to make 6 gallons (if possible) and stir in corn sugar.
2. Bring to a rolling boil and add boiling hops. 15 minutes before end of boil, add Irish Moss. After one hour's boil, turn off heat, stir in finishing hops, and cover. Let the wort rest one hour.
3. Strain off wort into primary fermenter. Remove one quart for yeast starter: top up primary to 5 gallons, cover, and force cool. Meanwhile, force cool starter wort and, when cooled to about 90°F, stir in yeast, plus a pinch of yeast energizer.
4. When wort is cool (70°F), stir up the starter and pitch it into the wort. Add ½ teaspoon yeast energizer, re-cover, and put in a cool place (60–68°F).
5. Let the ale ferment. When fermentation starts to slow down (2–3 days), skim the head. Skim again 24 hours later and rack into secondary. Add ½ teaspoon yeast energizer. Fit airlock. After 2 days, dissolve gelatine finings in 1 cup water and add.
6. When fermentation is over (no drop in specific gravity for five days), rack the beer back into primary, add ascorbic acid, make up priming syrup and add. Terminal gravity should be about 4 to

7 *before* adding priming syrup. Bottle and let it age 2 weeks before sampling. At 4 weeks it should be fully aged.

EXTRACT DIET LAGER

Most extract beers are really diet beers, with a low starting gravity (under 40), low terminal gravity (under 8), and low alcohol content. If this type of beer interests you, you may as well make it from extract.

Ingredients

2½–3 lbs. American Light malt extract
1½–1 lb. corn sugar (total of 4 lb. extract plus sugar)
1 teaspoon gypsum
¾ oz. Cascade or Cluster hops (boil)
¼ oz. same type hops (finishing)
1 teaspoon Irish Moss (optional)
1 packet lager yeast
Yeast energizer
1 teaspoon gelatine finings
1 teaspoon Ascorbic Acid
1⅓ cups corn sugar (priming)

Method

1. Dissolve extract and gypsum in one gallon hot water in the boiler. Top up to six gallons (if possible) and stir in sugar.
2. Bring to a rolling boil and add boiling hops. Boil an hour or more, adding Irish Moss 15 minutes before the end. When hour is over, turn off heat, stir in finishing hops, and cover. Let the wort rest one hour.
3. Strain off wort into primary. Remove one quart for starter, top primary up to 5 gallons, cover and force cool. Meanwhile, force cool starter wort to 80°F and add a pinch of yeast energizer, plus the yeast.
4. When wort is cool (70°F) stir up the starter and pitch it into the wort. Add ½ teaspoon of yeast energizer, re-cover and put in a very cool place – 50–55°F is best.

5. Let the beer ferment. Skim the head several times during primary fermentation. When fermentation slows down (gravity drop of only one or two points in 48 hours), rack to secondary and add ½ teaspoon yeast energizer. Fit airlock. 2 days later add finings dissolved in 1 cup warm water.
6. At end of fermentation (no gravity drop for five days) rack into primary, add ascorbic acid, make up syrup with priming sugar and add; then bottle. Terminal gravity should be 2 to 4 before adding priming syrup. Bottle and age one to two months.

ADAPTING GRAIN BEER RECIPES

While your results will suffer, it is possible to adapt any of the full-bodied grain beer recipes in Chapters Eleven and Twelve to extract simply by substituting pale malt extract for pale lager malt. I recommend American malt extract for pale lagers, because it is light in color. British extract is better for ales and dark lagers. Substitute as follows:

For adjuncts (corn or rice), substitute corn sugar pound for pound. For grain malt, substitute one pound of British extract or one and a quarter pounds of American extract for every pound and a half of malt.

Also remember that crystal and roasted malts, if needed, must be crushed with a rolling pin and added to the boiler. To get the full flavor from them, you should boil them for a full hour; then, after pouring off the hot bitter wort through the strainer, rinse out the boiler with a gallon of hot water and pour it through the strainer also. Even with this rinse you may not get *all* the goodness from the grains, so you may have to increase the amounts of roasted grain in the recipe.

Chapter 6

EQUIPMENT FOR GRAIN BEER BREWING

Since grain beers involve some extra work, it should not be surprising that they also require some extra equipment. The number of items is not large, but a few require some ingenuity and "leg work" to find or make.

Corona grain mill at work.

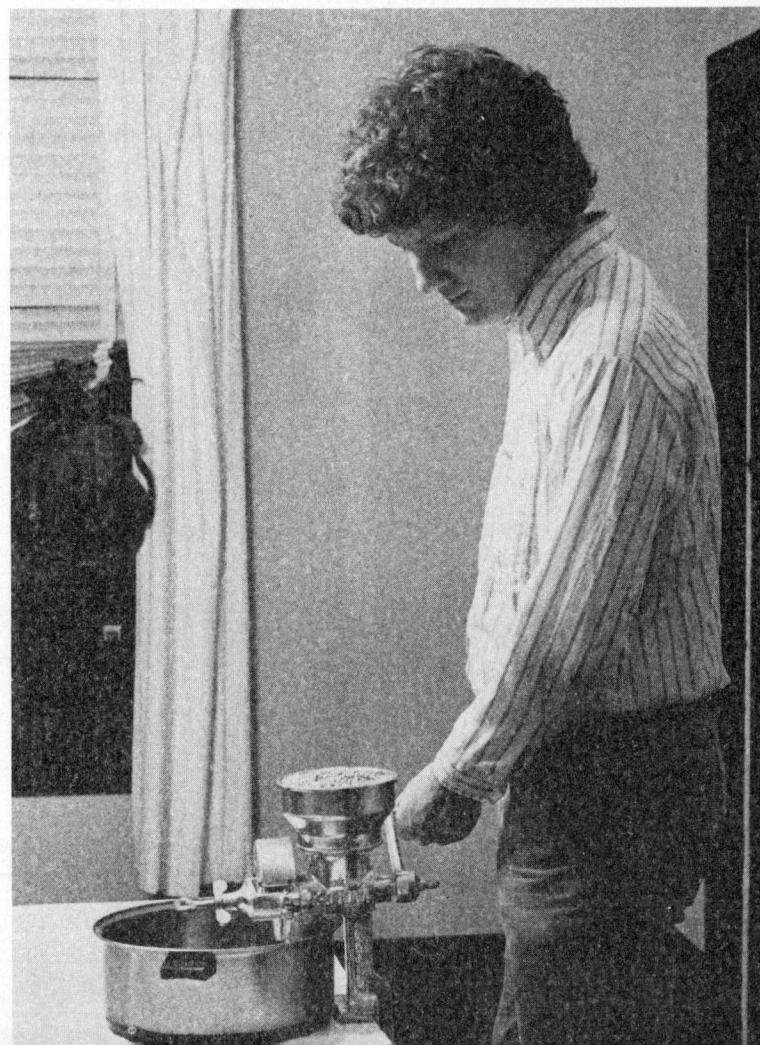

Grinder. From long, bitter experience, I advise you *never* to use either a blender or coffee grinder to grind your malt. Instead, buy a Corona grain mill, available from health food stores either locally or by mail. Be sure to wash it thoroughly before its first use, and use plenty of detergent to remove all traces of the packing grease; then rinse well to remove all traces of detergent.

Kettle. Your boiler can double as your mash kettle, but it is more convenient to have a separate vessel. Materials are the same as for boilers – stainless steel, copper or enamelware. A four-gallon capacity is minimum, and no lid is required.

Cereal Cooker. For boiling rice and other raw grain adjuncts, you need a second *covered* pot. I use a two-gallon aluminum spaghetti cooker; a three-gallon enamel pot would be better, and the larger capacity is really necessary for brewing American-style beers. Note that for all-malt beers, this pot is not needed.

Grain Bag and Lauter Tub. To strain the sweet wort from the grain husks, you need a sturdy plastic bucket of at least six gallons' capacity. You must fit it with a plastic faucet (available from winemaker' stores) installing it as close to the bottom as possible. Seal the joint with clear silicone rubber caulk, such as General Electric RTV.

The grain bag should be made to be a good fit inside the lauter tub. The sides should be of canvas, which is available at fabric stores. Also at fabric stores you can get a hundred yards of very heavy nylon thread and a sail needle to sew the thing up.

The bottom of the grain bag should be of sturdy mesh or screening material (fabric or plastic, *not* metal) with a mesh size of one-eighth to one-quarter inch. I found at a local discount store a large zippered bag of heavy nylon mesh, intended for washing pantyhose and other delicate items in the washing machine. I cut it apart and it yielded enough material for two grain bag bottoms. Another possible source of mesh would be a store that sells fish netting material. Look under "Nets" in the Yellow Pages.

I cannot turn this into a sewing book. Make your measurements and draw up your plans, leaving allowance for overlap at the seams.

Double check all your figures. Then buy your materials, mark and cut carefully, and finally ask your wife/girl friend/mother to teach you a basic interlocking stitch, and also how to tie ends. Remember, the bag need not be pretty, but it must be strong. Wherever there will be stress, use a double row of stitches.

The lauter tub also needs some kind of false bottom to hold the grain bag bottom away from the faucet. An old saucepan lid, minus its handle, will do. I use an aluminum false bottom intended for a pressure cooker.

Basic mash equipment: Left, *cereal cooker;* center, *mash kettle (four gallon capacity) sitting on the grain bag;* right, *lauter tub. Note the mesh bottom of the grain bag.*

OTHER MASHING SYSTEMS

A simple way out of your equipment problems is to purchase an insulated mash tun with a built in spigot and false bottom, which can thus serve as a lauter tub as well. The arrangement seems ideal, if more expensive, and my only objection to it is that it cannot be put on a stove. For mashing lager malt, some way must be found of boosting the mash temperature. Decoction mashing is the only solution, but it can be tricky. It requires removing a portion of the mash from the main vessel, bringing it to a boil, then returning it to the rest of the mash in order to raise the temperature. I feel that my mashing system is really easier to control, and since the mash is never boiled, no enzymes are destroyed and the whole process is faster. Since the equipment is also less costly, the only disadvantage is the time and effort required to make a lauter tub and grain bag.

If you should decide on a "ready made" system, follow the instructions carefully and *never*, under any circumstances, expose the mash tun to any direct source of heat. Better to lose a five dollar mash than a forty dollar mash tun.

Chapter 7

MAKING SWEET WORT FROM GRAIN MALT

I. GRINDING THE MALT

The object of grinding is to expose the powdery interior of the malt grain so that the enzymes and starches can be released into the mash water. A proper grind will leave most of the husks in large pieces – *not* powdered. In fact, the best grind is the coarsest grind which does not leave any grains of malt intact.

As a starting point, I suggest setting the adjusting screw of the Corona grain mill by first turning it until it just begins to push against the outer grinding disc. Then grind about a cup of malt and examine it, and tighten if necessary.

Measuring the grain can be difficult without a kitchen scale, since the volume of a pound can vary. One solution is to measure out two volumes of eight ounces each on your hop scale, then combine them in a one-quart pyrex measuring pitcher. From this you can directly read the volume of a pound of your malt.

It is very smart to grind your malt the night before a brewing session. The Corona mill is efficient, but it is still tiresome to crank six to nine pounds of grain through it. You will start brewing in a better frame of mind if you get some sleep after finishing this chore.

II. WATER TREATMENT

One of the most confusing aspects of home brewing is water treatment. It is possible to go into almost endless detail on the subject, and to try to duplicate different water supplies from famous brewing cities such as Munich or Dortmund. I have found that this duplication is not always possible unless you start with distilled water, and it is not usually worth the trouble, because so many other things – such as the type of malt – have a much greater effect on the taste of beer. However, the *wrong* water supply can harm the flavor a great deal; so in this section I will be pointing out what good brewing water should, and should not, contain.

Claims are sometimes made for the importance of water to a good starch conversion. I have not found water to be critical, at least with American malt; it is so loaded with diastase that almost *any* water will work, as long as it is reasonably neutral.

From my experience, all beers can be placed into two categories: dark and light (or pale). Similarly, water can be called either hard or soft, depending upon whether it contains a great deal of calcium and sulfate (gypsum). Hard, neutral water is good for making pale beers. The sulfate seems to mellow the hop flavor, while the calcium promotes a good enzyme action. Soft, neutral water is good for making dark beers, which do not need the benefits of gypsum.

Hard, neutral water is made by adding gypsum to soft, neutral water. *No other compounds* – including table salt – should ever be added to brewing water; they can only harshen the flavor of the finished beer. This being the case, the home brewer needs to get hold of two things: some gypsum, and a supply of soft, neutral water. Fortunately, most tap water provides a good starting point; but it is usually alkaline. To neutralize it, you must first find out what it contains. This means a telephone call to your water company.

Water Analysis

You should not be intimidated by talking to a chemist. Once you explain what you are doing, he will be happy to help. However, you must understand the analysis he will give you. This requires a little "brushing up" on basic chemistry.

Strictly speaking, there are no salts (such as gypsum or table salt) in water. There are only ions. When you dissolve a teaspoon of gypsum into your brewing water, the compound ionizes – breaks up – into electrically charged particles, or *ions*, of calcium and sulfate.

Since there are only ions in water, you cannot ask a chemist how much gypsum there is in your water supply. The question cannot be answered. What you need to know is the ion content, measured in *parts per million* (ppm). Ask for the content of the following ions: Calcium (Ca); Sodium (Na); Magnesium (Mg); Carbonate and bicarbonate (usually lumped together in analysis "as CO_3"); Nitrate (NO_3); Sulfate (SO_4); and chloride (Cl). All of these ions can, in different ways, affect your beer; the biggest problems are large amounts – over 100 ppm – of sodium or nitrate.

Besides ion content, you also need to know the treatment given at the plant. All water companies filter and sterilize their water. Many add fluoride (which is harmless) and chlorine, which is a disinfecting gas and not at all the same as chloride *ion*. Chlorine is usually harmless, but if too much is added, the water will have a swimming pool smell. If this is true of your water, simply draw your water a few days before brewing and let it stand in an open vessel; the gas will come out of the solution by itself.

Far more critical, as far as brewing is concerned, are the other chemical treatments that may be used. Many water companies add lime to get rid of bicarbonates and thus prevent chalk build-up in the pipes. Lime-treated water is fine for brewing, but it is very alkaline and must be neutralized before use.

WATER
TREATMENT

Water treatment supplies for mashing: Measuring spoons, gypsum, concentrated lactic acid, small test tube, indicator solution. Resting in front is the color chart used with the indicator solution to find the actual pH of the brewing water. In the large bottle is dilute lactic acid, used to neutralize the brewing water. (See text.)

Some waters are also treated with soda ash to get rid of other ions. This treatment leaves a large amount of sodium ion in the water, and such water is *not* suitable for brewing. Ask the water company if you could collect your water at the plant prior to the soda-ash treatment.

Water not treated with either lime or soda ash will probably have a fair amount of carbonate – over 75 ppm. If this is the case, the water can be boiled for half an hour. The carbonate will precipitate as chalk around the rim and bottom of the boiler. After cooling, you can siphon off the soft, neutral water for brewing.

If your water is naturally high in sodium or nitrate, you may have to distill your water or find another source. Assuming that you do not face this problem, there are two ways to get soft, neutral water. Which you need to use depends on your water supply.

1) If the water is lime-treated, neutralize it. Get a pH test kit from a tropical fish store. Make up a dilute acid solution by dissolving one and a half teaspoons of citric acid or two teaspoons of 88% lactic acid in 24 fluid ounces of water. Add this dilute acid to nine gallons of tap water, one teaspoon at a time, until the pH is brought down to seven (neutrality).

2) If the water has not been lime-treated, boil it and rack as described above.

A word on home water softeners: These "soften" water by exchanging calcium and magnesium ion for sodium. The end result is bad brewing water. If you have a home softener, draw off your brewing water *before* it goes into the machine.

If you want dark beer, you need soft, neutral water. However, pale or light beers need hard water. To figure how much gypsum you need to harden your water, the formula is as follows:

Perfectly soft (distilled) water would need four and a half teaspoons of gypsum for nine gallons. For every eighty (80) ppm of sulfate already in your water, subtract one teaspoon from this figure. For example, my local water contains about 120 ppm of sulfate. 120 divided by 80 gives 1.5, or one and a half teaspoons of gypsum. I subtract this amount from the starting figure, and so find that I must add three teaspoons of gypsum to make my hard, neutral water.

You should *not* add the total amount of gypsum to the nine gallons of water. Instead, first measure out the amount of mash water (see the recipe) into your kettle. Then add half the gypsum, or one and a half teaspoons, which ever amount is greater. The remaining gypsum, if any, is added to the boiler after sparging.

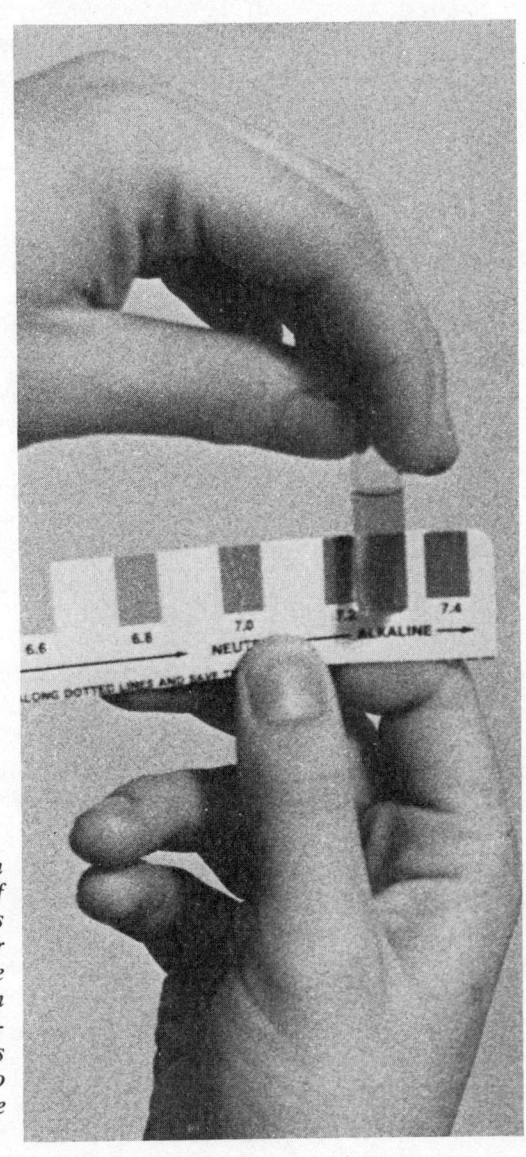

Using the color comparison chart to determine the pH of water. Before the picture was taken, one drop of indicator solution was added to the half-vial of tap water. When neutralizing, add dilute lactic or citric acid until pH falls to 7. (Neutrality.) note: Do not return the water sample to the vat after testing!

That is all there is to it. To recapitulate, the steps in water treatment are:

First, a call to the water company – this need only be done once;

Second, make "soft, neutral water" by either neutralizing limed water or boiling and racking water that has not been limed;

Third, measure out your mash water and add gypsum in the required amount, and add more, if needed, at the boiling stage.

One question which may arise here is, "What if my water contains so much sulfate that it is what you call 'hard' already?" You can of course make pale beer with this water. Such water is not ideal for dark beer, but you can still use it. Dark beer made from hard water will probably be a little drier (low terminal gravity) and less bitter than the same beer made from soft water. If your first batch comes out that way, it is simple to adjust your procedures and recipes to compensate.

The real problem waters, as I said above, are those containing nitrate, which harms yeast, or sodium, which gives a bad flavor. Magnesium also gives a bad taste, but it takes more of it to do this.

Any of these ions, in large concentrations, means trouble. Distillation is an expensive remedy. If you know someone who has a deep well, have some of its water analyzed – it is usually good for brewing even in parts of the country where the surface water is almost brackish.

III. COOKING CEREAL ADJUNCTS

If your recipe calls for no adjuncts, or if you have them in pre-cooked form (flakes), skip this section. Pre-cooking of adjuncts adds time to a brewing session, and for amateurs, the amount of money saved is negligible. In fact, flakes are more expensive than malt. It follows that the only reason for using adjuncts is to modify the taste and color of the finished beer.

Whether your adjunct is rice, corn, or barley, the cooking process is similar. First, wash the cereal thoroughly. Put it in a large pot, add a gallon of water, stir thoroughly, and then pour off the water through a strainer. Repeat five times or more, until the water poured off is just as clean as the water that went in. After the last rinse, drain completely.

Next, fill your cereal cooker with a part or all of your mash water:

three quarts per pound of cereal, or the full amount, whichever is less. Bring the water to a boil over full heat with the lid off. Once the water starts to boil, stir, then cover the pot and turn down the heat so that the cereal is boiling gently. Stir every five to ten minutes to minimize sticking.

Cooking time depends upon the adjunct. Corn grits cook fastest, barley slowest, with rice falling in between. The cereal is done when it *gelatinizes*. At this point the starch has absorbed the maximum amount of water and is evenly dispersed in a semiclear, gluey mixture. Individual grains and husks, representing the non-starchy fraction of the grain, may still be visible, but the gelatinized state is unmistakable. When you see it, turn off the heat and transfer the cooked cereal to the mash kettle. Some starch will be stuck to the bottom of the pot. This is normal, and if you have stirred frequently, it should not be much. Do not attempt to scrape up more than will come off easily.

Supplies and equipment for grain beer: Thermometer, resting against the cereal cooker; mash kettle, sitting on the grain bag; and lauter tub. To the left, in front of the cereal cooker, are water treatment supplies: indicator solution, test tube, concentrated lactic acid, and resting in front of these, the color chart used to find the pH of the brewing water. The wine bottle holds dilute lactic acid. (See text.)

Finally, stir to mix the gelatinized mass with the rest of the mash water and let it cool to 125°F. You are now ready to begin the mash.

IV. MASHING

The purpose of mashing is twofold: to reduce the haze-forming malt proteins to simpler forms which can be "boiled out" of solution; and to convert the malt and adjunct starch into sugar. These things cannot be accomplished simultaneously. Protein enzymes are active from about 95 to 125 degrees; the starch enzymes from about 135 to 155 degrees. Thus the mashing of lager malt calls for a two-temperature system. The grain is mashed in at 125°F and held between 118° and 122° for a one-half to one hour "protein rest"; then the temperature is boosted to 155°F and held between there and 150° for starch conversion.

The time required for each stage depends on the concentration of enzymes in the mash kettle. American malt is rich in enzymes, but adjuncts are devoid of them; thus, the more adjuncts in the mash kettle, the longer each stage of the mash must be. The exception to this rule is the protein rest, because corn and rice are very low in protein and will lower the protein content of the finished beer.

One of the beauties of lager malt is the opportunity it affords for controlling the sweetness of the finished beer. This ability is a natural result of the high enzyme content; to understand it, we must look at the starch conversion process.

Starch is converted by two enzymes called *alpha* and *beta amylase*. They are sometimes lumped together and called *diastase*, but they are different chemicals and do different jobs. Alpha amylase converts starch into complex sugars called *dextrins*, which are largely unfermentable by yeast. Thus they remain in the finished beer and give it its malty sweetness. Alpha amylase works best at high temperatures (around 150°F) and can withstand temperatures in excess of 163°F. Beta amylase converts dextrins to *maltose*, a simple sugar which is totally fermentable. Beta amylase works best at 135° to 150°F; at high temperatures it is slowly destroyed.

Another factor which affects enzyme performance is the pH (acidity) of the mash. Beta amylase prefers a low pH (around 5.0), while alpha amylase works best at a higher pH (around 5.6).

These differences mean that it is possible to control the ratio of dextrins to maltose in the wort by controlling the factors involved. A low-temperature, low-pH mash will favor beta amylase and a high proportion of maltose. This means that the finished beer will be less sweet and have a low specific gravity. Conversely, a high-temperature, high-pH mash will favor alpha amylase and dextrin production, and a sweet, high-gravity beer will result.

In practice, it is hard to control pH precisely, and my technique is based on temperature. It has a good deal of latitude, since a mistake of five degrees is seldom serious if corrected. Your very first mash should produce a good-tasting beer, even if the sweetness is not exactly as specified. The only place you have to be careful is in the high-temperature stage, where you should make every effort to avoid exceeding 155°F. An "overshoot" may kill off the beta amylase prematurely, so don't be too eager to pour on the heat. Follow the procedure for temperature checks and be patient.

Mashing Technique

Step 1. Bring the mash water, or mash water and cooked cereal, to 125°F. Add the ground malt in stages and stir thoroughly to disperse it. Make sure there are no "dry lumps". If necessary, add a little more water to get a very thick, but stirrable "porridge". Extra water should only be needed if a good deal of mash water has been boiled off while cooking the adjuncts.

Step 2. After ten minutes, check the temperature. Whenever you do this, remember that thermometers respond slowly and must be given time to read accurately. Hold the thermometer with the bulb half way down in the mash, and move it alongside the spoon as you stir thoroughly for thirty seconds. Then return the thermometer to the center of the pot, still half way down, and read it. This procedure should give you a true average reading.

Step 3. Check the temperature every ten minutes. When it drops to 118°F, boost it back up to 122 by applying the heat on full for two minutes, stirring constantly. Turn off the heat and stir for another thirty seconds before checking the temperature. If you are within a degree or two, apply the heat for only a minute; if you have only boosted the temperature by one degree, increase the "heat on" time to three or four minutes. Then recheck, remembering to stir for thirty seconds with the heat off first. Continue the cycle of ten-minute checks until the protein rest time is up.

Step 4. This is the *boost* to starch conversion temperature, and is accomplished in three stages.
a) Apply the heat on full for two to four minutes, depending on the heat output of your stove. Then turn off the heat and stir as always for thirty seconds before checking the temperature. Repeat until the mash has been raised to 140°F.
b) Let it rest at 140° for three to ten minutes, depending on the recipe.
Example: Your recipe says, boost the mash temperature from 122 to 155 degrees in fifteen minutes. If the boost from 122° to 140° took five minutes, you can assume that the boost from 140° to 155° will also take five minutes. So, 5 minutes (first half of boost) plus 5 minutes (second half of boost) equals ten minutes total. Since the total time for this step is 15 minutes, you should let the mash rest at 140° for five minutes, and the total time should then come out to fifteen minutes. An error of a minute or two will not make much difference.
c) Boost the rest of the way to 155°F, using the procedure outlined in (a).

Step 5. During the high-temperature starch conversion step, check the mash every three minutes, and when it drops to 150°, boost it *slowly* back to 155°, applying full heat for only two minutes at a time. Don't forget to stir.

Step 6. When starch conversion time is over, boost the temperature quickly to 168°F. You may apply full heat for up to five minutes at a time. Let the mash stand at 168° for at least five minutes, and then transfer it to the lauter tub.
   The reason for the boost to 168° is to deliberately kill off all the beta amylase and thus stabilize the ratio of dextrins to maltose. Without this step, the beta amylase would continue to break down dextrins and the result would be a dry, thin beer.

Straining the hot wort out after boiling.

As you can see, the major controls of beer sweetness (terminal gravity) are the length of the boost step and the length of the high temperature rest. Shortening either or both will favor alpha amylase and a sweeter finished beer.

The times given in the recipe should give a terminal gravity which is appropriate for the type of beer. If, on your first attempt, they do not, adjust your mashing times as needed.

I must warn you that there are limits to these controls. The heat output of any stove burner is limited, and this means that the boost will require a certain minimum amount of time – usually ten minutes or so. Also, at least twenty minutes at 150–155°F are required to convert all the starch. These minimum times mean that, while sweetness can be controlled, you cannot make an all-dextrin or even a half-dextrin wort. Beyond a certain point, the only way to get a sweeter beer is to use more grain.

Electric Stoves

I use a gas stove. The slow heat-up and cool-down times of electric burner elements make temperature control difficult. I suggest that, instead of turning the heat on and off, you try leaving the largest front burner on full or high heat; then, instead of removing the heat from the mash, remove the mash from the heat by transferring it to the other (cold) front burner. This is the same as shutting off the flame on a gas stove. Be very careful of the hot element, though: do not wear loose clothing or get anything flammable (such as your hair) near the stove. If you have small children, never leave your kitchen during a mash session.

V. SPARGING

The object of sparging is to separate the liquid malt sugar solution (sweet wort) from the grain husks. This is necessary because boiling the whole mass of grain would be very awkward. Also, the husks would give an off flavor to the finished beer.

This is not to say that you cannot let *any* grain husks or debris through into the boiler. But though a small amount will do no harm, the less, the better.

During the 168 degree rest at the end of mashing, you should fit your false bottom into the lauter tub, making sure that it sits on top of the faucet fitting, so as to hold the grain bag away from the faucet opening. Then insert the grain bag into the lauter tub, and try to fit the sides as close to the tub as possible. A few spring clothespins may help to keep the top of the bag wide open.

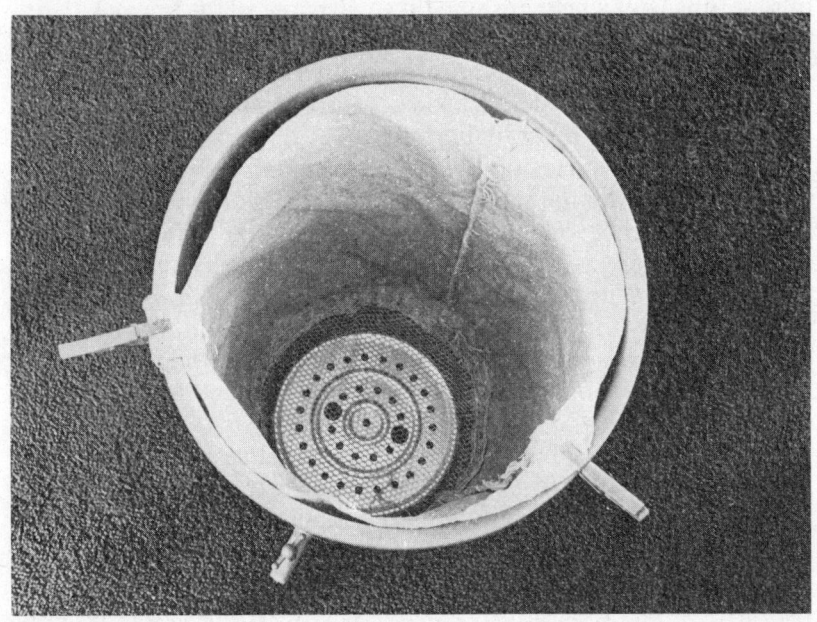

Grain bag in place in the lauter tub. Note the clothespins holding the sides; also the false bottom; and the double stitching of the bottom and side seams.

After transferring the hot, sweet mash to the lauter tub, be sure to scrape any debris still remaining in the kettle on to the top of the grain mass. Then fill the kettle with about half your sparge water (2½–3 gallons), and heat it to around 165°F. If you have a cereal cooker, you can heat half your sparge water during the mash; this saves time as you can sparge with this water while the remainder is heating in the mash kettle. Otherwise, as sparge water is removed from the kettle, add more cold neutral water and apply heat to keep the temperature between 160° and 170°F.

When the sparge water is ready, you can begin. Place your boiler under the lauter tub spigot. Then hold a one gallon jug or soup pot directly under the tap to catch the first, cloudy runnings. Open the tap slowly until the wort starts to flow. It will probably sputter at first and you may have to close and re-open the tap to "push through" a grain husk blocking the flow.

Once the wort is flowing, try to let it just trickle out. This is maddening, but a fast, gushing flow will carry all the fine powdered debris down deep into the grain mass, and pack that mass very tightly together. This condition is known as a "set mash" and is worth avoiding. The ideal is a loosely packed mass, which demands a slow flow during the initial runoff.

As the sweet wort is drawn off, the grain mass begins to form a filter bed and trap the smaller particles. The wort will slowly begin to clear, though it will never become crystal clear. After a couple of quarts have been run off, the wort should be clean enough for you to remove the jug or pot and let the wort flow straight into the boiler. Now is the time to open the tap as far as it will go. Next, *gently* return the cloudy wort to the surface of the grains – just trickle it over them – and do not let the liquid get higher than the surface.

If your filter bed has been loosely packed as specified, all you have to do now is keep gently trickling hot sparge water all over the surface of the grain, maintaining the liquid level just below it. As the sparge water is removed, do not forget to add more.

When all the water has been poured through, let the last runnings drain off naturally. Do *not* press the grains or tilt the lauter tub. One way to save time is to put your *clean* cereal cooker under the tub to collect the last couple of gallons. Bringing the first fraction to a boil takes around half an hour, so you can save that much time by collecting the last couple of gallons separately and adding it to the first runnings while they are on the stove.

In any case, after the wort is all run off you must dispose of the spent grains. Close the tap before carrying your lauter tub to the kitchen sink. There, remove the grain bag and squeeze out the grains before dumping them into a plastic bag. Finally, carefully rinse the grain bag, inside and out, with plenty of hot water, and hang it up to dry. Wash out the lauter tub and set it aside to dry. You can also wash the mash kettle and other items during the boil.

Equipment set up for sparging.

Set Mash

Mashing may be the most complicated part of brewing, but sparging a set mash is the biggest pain. If you cannot or do not get a loose grain pack, the wort flow may slow to a trickle or even stop altogether as the first runnings are drawn off. As long as they continue to run, I would advise that you recirculate all the sweet, cloudy wort before trying to unclog the set. The basic procedure is to close the tap and stir the mash, adding enough sparge water to keep the liquid level even with the grain. There are two variations on the basic method.

1) Stir the whole mash thoroughly, deliberately breaking up the entire grain pack. This means starting all over and this time letting the first runnings drain off slowly.

2) If you have a tricky spigot or grain that is ground too fine, starting over may not help. In this case the best procedure is to stir the grain, but be careful to leave the bottom inch or two firmly packed. Top up the water level as before.

In this instance you need only collect a pint or so from the initial surge when the tap is re-opened. After returning this, gently add more sparge water. Gradually raise the water level over the top of the grain mass, and see whether the flow becomes faster as the water level is raised (it should). If this happens, and the wort continues to run clear, you can add up to a gallon of water over the original grain level in order to keep up a fast flow of wort. The fine ground debris will rise to the surface and float there, but this is of no concern. However, do not become careless and add water so fast that it breaks up the densely packed filter layer at the bottom of the bag.

For really desperate cases, you may need this final remedy: Forget about recirculating and just let the debris wash through; when the mash sets, stir it while pouring sparge water through. The stirring will force the water through, but a large amount of debris will also wash into the boiler. Finally, when all the wort is collected, transfer it to your primary and place it, covered, on a high shelf or table. After an hour or two the grain debris will have settled out and you can rack the clean wort back into the boiler. Do not move the racking tube around on the bottom of the primary or try to tilt it. Insert it as gently as you can and hold the top so that it cannot move while you are starting the siphon. You will lose a quart or so of wort at the bottom, but your beer will be saved. Remember – try the other methods first. This one should not be necessary unless you have ground your malt in a blender.

Chapter 8

MAKING BITTER WORT (BOILING)

Boiling completely destroys all enzymes and sterilizes the sweet wort. Just as important is the fact that it extracts the resins from the hops. But it has yet another function: to clarify the beer.

Sweet wort is reasonably clear, but contains fine particles of protein which give it a slight haze. During boiling, these proteins coagulate into larger and larger clumps, which can then settle out and leave the wort crystal clear. This coagulation is called the "hot break" and usually takes about an hour to complete. A good hot break will leave the wort sparkling.

The hot break can be improved by adding Irish Moss during the last fifteen minutes of the boil. It should be used in all pale beers.

Management of the boil requires some experience. It takes a lot of heat to bring six gallons of wort to a boil, but once it starts, foam will build up with appalling speed, and boilovers are part of every home brewer's initiation into his art.

The quickest way to stop a boilover is to remove the lid. The boiler must be kept covered to minimize heat loss, but you should never cover a boiler completely. Leave a space an inch wide toward the front so that you can see the surface of the wort. Foam will start to well up before the rolling boil begins, and this is your cue to pull the lid off a little further and check the kettle frequently.

The boiling time only begins when the wort starts to kick and roll. This agitation is just as important as the heat in coagulating the proteins; so, contrary to some recipes, wort must always be boiled, rather than merely simmered.

An hour before the end of the boiling time (given in the recipe), loose hops and compressed hops should be added to the wort. The latter should be broken up first. Pelletized hops can also be added at this time; however, because they are finely powdered, pelletized hops do not need a full hour's boil to release their bitter resins. Ten minutes are enough; and if you add your pelletized hops during the last ten minutes only, you can reduce or eliminate the quota of finishing hops. However, you may still want to dry hop for more aroma.

Do not forget to add Irish Moss fifteen minutes before the end of the boil. Then, when the time is up, turn off the heat and stir in the finishing hops. Cover completely to prevent the escape of volatile aromatic substances, and let the wort rest for an hour.

Toward the end of the rest period, put two quarts of soft, neutral water into a teapot and bring to a boil. Then suspend a plastic colander over your primary and line it with cheesecloth (eight layers) or mosquito netting (four layers). Use clothespins to hold this filter in place.

When the rest period is over, pour off the clear, hot wort through the colander into the primary. Work slowly and cautiously to avoid spills. When all the wort is poured off, empty the remaining hops-plus-break-protein sediment into the colander. Then pour the teakettle full of boiling water into the boiler and swirl it around. Finally, pour it through the colander, moving the stream all over the surface in order to rinse as much sugar as possible from the spent hops.

If necessary, the primary should now be topped up to the five gallon mark with brewing water; then add one more quart, and stir. Then *remove* one quart to a half-gallon jug, and place it in a sink full of cold water to force cool. This will become your starter (see the next Chapter). The rest of the wort should be set in a bathtub full of cold water and covered.

The object of forced cooling is to bring the wort down to room temperature as quickly as possible. This minimizes the risk of infection, and also helps the "cold break". As the wort cools, more proteins will clump together and become visible. Thus the clear wort will become cloudy once more. Do not be alarmed; all proteins which coagulate during the cold break will eventually drop out. In fact, a good cold break is just as important as the hot break to the clarity of the beer.

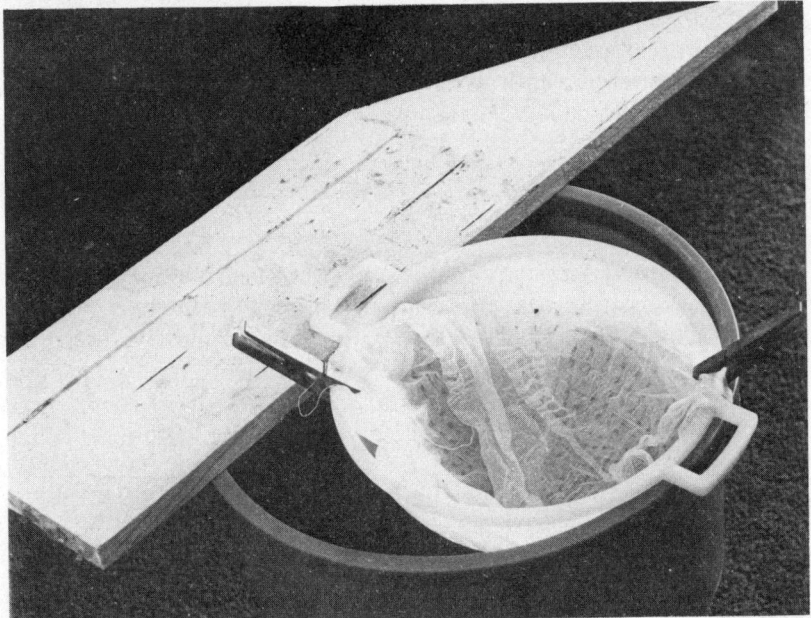

Primary with strainer suspended over it, ready to receive the hot bitter wort after boiling. Note the mosquito netting used as a filter element in the strainer.

HYDROMETER READING

The last step before fermentation is to assess the effectiveness of your mash. When your wort is cool, you will find that it has "shrunk" slightly, so top it back up to five gallons. Stir well, then fill your hydrometer jar and take a reading. Spin the instrument to dislodge any bubbles, then "eyeball" your reading straight across the surface of the wort. Ignore the little curvature of the liquid where it seems to ride up the stem. Make sure you are looking at the *Specific Gravity* (S.G.) scale, and record your reading. Pour back the wort and rinse out the jar.

To be certain of your accuracy, you should double-check the hydrometer by floating it in plain water at 60°F. It should read zero. If it is higher, read off where it floats and use that as a negative (minus) correction factor for your readings. My hydrometer reads three (1.003) in sixty-degree tap water, so I have to subtract three points from all my readings. Finally, you must apply the temperature correction given in the instructions that came with your hydrometer. Only when both corrections (if needed) have been made will you have an accurate idea of the starting or original gravity of your wort.

DEGREES OF EXTRACT

You are now in a position to assess your mash and malt. Most of my recipes assume that a pound of malt yields thirty *degrees of extract*. This is the gravity of one gallon of wort made by mashing one pound of lager malt. Thus, five gallons of wort made from eight pounds of malt should have a starting gravity of 30 (degrees of extract) times 8 (pounds of malt) divided by five (gallons), which equals 48.

The extract you get may be higher or lower than thirty. Knowing the extract you can get will enable you to adjust your recipes to get the starting gravity you want.

However, under no circumstances should you add corn sugar to grain beer wort in order to make up for a low extract. To do so would actually lower your final gravity, and make it impossible to assess or adjust your mashing technique. Terminal gravity has more effect on flavor than the alcohol content of the beer, so never do anything to distort it.

Chapter 9

FERMENTATION

Many beer books give more attention to fermentation than to any other stage of brewing. I must say that, in my experience, it is the easiest, most trouble-free part of the whole process. The yeast does the work, and all you have to do is skim and rack. I have never had a "stuck fermentation" and I doubt that you will, either. I also believe that too much attention to many wrinkles in the fermentation process only distracts the home brewer from putting his time and attention into other steps in the process which make a lot more difference in the final result. Learning to mash will enable you to improve your home brew far more than any change you could make in the basic fermentation method.

One way to assure a successful fermentation is to make a *starter*.

Yeast starter ready for pitching. Note foam on top, and layer of yeast at bottom of jug. Always stir the starter before pitching, to make sure you get all the yeast into the batch of wort!

Take a quart of hot bitter wort and force cool it as rapidly as possible. When it reaches the temperature given on the yeast package, pitch in the yeast granules and swirl them around. While the main volume of wort is cooling, the yeast will be activated and begin to multiply. You will get as much as five times as much yeast as you started with, and your main batch will begin to ferment much more quickly as a result.

Once the wort is cooled to room temperature (60–68°F), swirl the starter vigorously to mix all the yeast in, then pitch it into the primary and stir thoroughly. The yeast will not begin to ferment immediately; it will first go through a growth, or *lag period* during which no activity can be seen. This is a nervous period for beginners. All you can do is keep the primary tightly covered and wait it out.

The first sign of fermentation is usually the appearance of small "islands" of white foam or grayish-tan break proteins on the surface of the brew. These can take anywhere from four to sixteen hours to appear. (Ale yeast starts much faster than lager yeast, which is one reason I recommend it for beginners.) As soon as you see these islands, move the beer to a cooler place, if possible: 60°F is ideal for ale yeast, 40–50°F for lager.

During the following 12 to 48 hours, fermentation will build to a furious peak. A thick layer of foam, mixed with large clumps of bitter break protein, yeast, and hop resins, will cover the brew. It is important to keep the head clean by skimming off all these bitter substances; otherwise, they may re-dissolve in the beer and give it an intensely harsh bitterness. Try to skim off only the dirty, contaminated parts of the head and leave the layer of clean foam intact.

As primary fermentation abates, the head will gradually become less dense, with bigger, frothier bubbles. This may happen anywhere from 18 to 96 hours after fermentation began. At this point be sure to skim the head carefully, as it may disappear in a matter of hours, dropping all the bitter contaminants back into the beer.

When the head has fallen, it is time to position the primary on a high table or chair and use your racking tube to siphon the beer into the secondary fermenter. Before siphoning, break up the dry hops (if necessary) and put them into the empty secondary. Also put in one-fourth cup of Polyclar, if you are using it.

During racking, try to keep the mouth of the hose below the level of beer in the secondary. This will minimize oxidation and foaming. Toward the end of racking, tilt the primary in order to recover as much beer as possible while still leaving the dregs behind.

Take a reading with your hydrometer and thermometer and record them. Fill the airlock to the proper level with water and attach.

If dry hops and/or Polyclar are used, the beer should be stirred twice a day for the first two days. After that, the secondary should be lifted and rotated, a quarter turn clockwise, then a quarter turn counterclockwise, once a day. The dry hops tend to float on the surface of the beer; rotating the carboy will force the hops down into the beer for maximum soaking and extraction of the hop oils. Seven to nine days of this treatment should be enough. The reason for the gentle rotation is to avoid stirring, which would prevent the yeast, and Polyclar, from settling out.

About five days before bottling – that is, after four to nine days in the secondary – the beer should be fined with gelatine. Put one-half cup of cold water in a small saucepan and sprinkle the gelatine on the surface: one teaspoon for ale yeast, one-half teaspoon for lager. Let it soak for half an hour, then heat gently while stirring to dissolve. *Do not boil.* Pour the finings solution into the secondary and stir gently to disperse it through the beer.

Two weeks in secondary is almost always enough. However, to be sure fermentation *is* over, take a hydrometer reading when you add finings, then five days later, before bottling. Even if the gravity is as high as fifteen, the beer may be finished. The test is whether the gravity has dropped over the five day period. If it has not, the beer is ready to bottle, regardless of gravity and even though there may still be a ring of bubbles on the surface of the beer.

ALCOHOL CONTENT

When fermentation is over, you can estimate the alcohol content of your beer as follows: first, subtract the terminal gravity from the starting gravity. Then, divide this number by 7.5. This will give you the percentage by volume of alcohol in your beer. Do not be upset if it is only four to five per cent: few American beers are over four per cent, and remember, the stronger the beer, the less you can drink at one time.

For example, if you brew a light lager with a starting gravity of fifty, and it ferments out to a final gravity of twelve (which is about right for most lagers), the gravity *drop* was 38 points. 38 divided by 7.5 gives an estimated 5% alcohol content, which is the legal limit for commercial domestic beers and (despite old wives' tales to the contrary) as strong as almost any imported beer as well.

Equipment set up for racking after first fermentation.

Chapter 10

BOTTLING, AGING AND SERVING

Next to a set mash, the biggest pain for a brewer is cleaning bottles. Unless they are rinsed out after use, beer bottles attract all kinds of disgusting phenomena, from cigarette butts and black fungi to waterbugs. You will probably find all these things in a typical case of "empty" beer bottles.

The basic procedure is to soak your bottles – 54 for a five gallon batch – in a bathtub full of warm water for a couple of hours. Use a windshield scraper and nylon scouring pad to get the labels off, and shake each bottle to dislodge anything loose inside it. Then hold it up to the light and actually look down to the bottom. If anything is still in there, use your "bottle washer" dowel rod (see Chapter Three) to get it off. Rinse the bottles with clean tap water, inside and out, and set to one side.

When all the bottles are clean and de-labeled, they should either be run through a dishwasher or put in chlorine detergent and then rinsed *thoroughly* in hot water *three times*. Dishwashers can be run with plain water – no detergent – because the hot water plus the heat-dry cycle will sterilize them adequately.

With your bottles washed, the worst is over. Rinse out your primary – you should, of course, have sterilized it after racking – and put one teaspoon of anti-oxidant (Vitamin C) or four powdered Campden tablets in the bottom. Rack the brew from the secondary back into the primary.

PRIMARY

In order to carbonate the beer, fermentation must take place in the sealed bottles; the carbon dioxide produced by this bottle fermentation is, of course, trapped, and so it dissolves in the beer. The "fuel" for this renewed fermentation is a small amount of corn sugar, which is added to the beer just before bottling. Generally, about six to eight ounces of corn sugar (one to one and a third cups) is used for a five gallon batch. This sugar is known as "priming".

The best way to add the corn sugar is to make up a syrup by removing a quart of beer from the secondary fermenter into a small saucepan. Heat it gently to about 150°F and stir in the priming sugar to dissolve. Then, just before bottling, pour this syrup back into the main batch of beer and stir well to disperse it. This method is less tedious than "dry priming", which requires adding a scant teaspoon of sugar to each bottle. It also ensures uniform carbonation, and allows fine adjustments in the level of carbonation. After the priming syrup has been added and thoroughly stirred into the main volume of the beer, bottle and cap *and label* a test bottle before adding heading compound. Place the primary on a high shelf or refrigerator and arrange the bottles on a table or counter below. Then assemble the racking tube and hose and start the siphon. As soon as the beer begins to flow, crimp the hose and attach the bottle filler. Fill each bottle in turn; you will have to fill the last few from a Pyrex pitcher. If you have a few ounces left over, use it to top-up some of your bottles to about an inch or so below the mouth of the bottle. NEVER cap a half-full bottle: the gas pressure inside will be enormous. Finally, cap all the bottles, rinse and wipe dry, and set them back in their cases. Clean everything, and you have made beer!

There is almost always enough yeast in the beer to get a bottle fermentation. If your beer is very clear, and you are worried, you can take one teaspoon of dregs from your secondary and stir it into the beer before bottling.

It takes at least ten days to carbonate the beer. During this time the bottles should be stored at fermentation temperature. After two weeks, you can try a sample to see what you have made. Chill the bottle in the refrigerator for five hours, then uncap and pour slowly into a glass. You must always do this in one motion; watch the bottle carefully, and when you see yeast starting to float up toward the mouth of the bottle, stop. The half inch or so left in the bottom is waste.

Well aged, naturally carbonated beers are regarded as having the finest head and flavor. The penalty you pay for these benefits is the fraction of each bottle which must be discarded. Be sure to empty all bottles and rinse thoroughly after serving your beer. Otherwise you will have a dried yeast deposit which is almost impossible to remove.

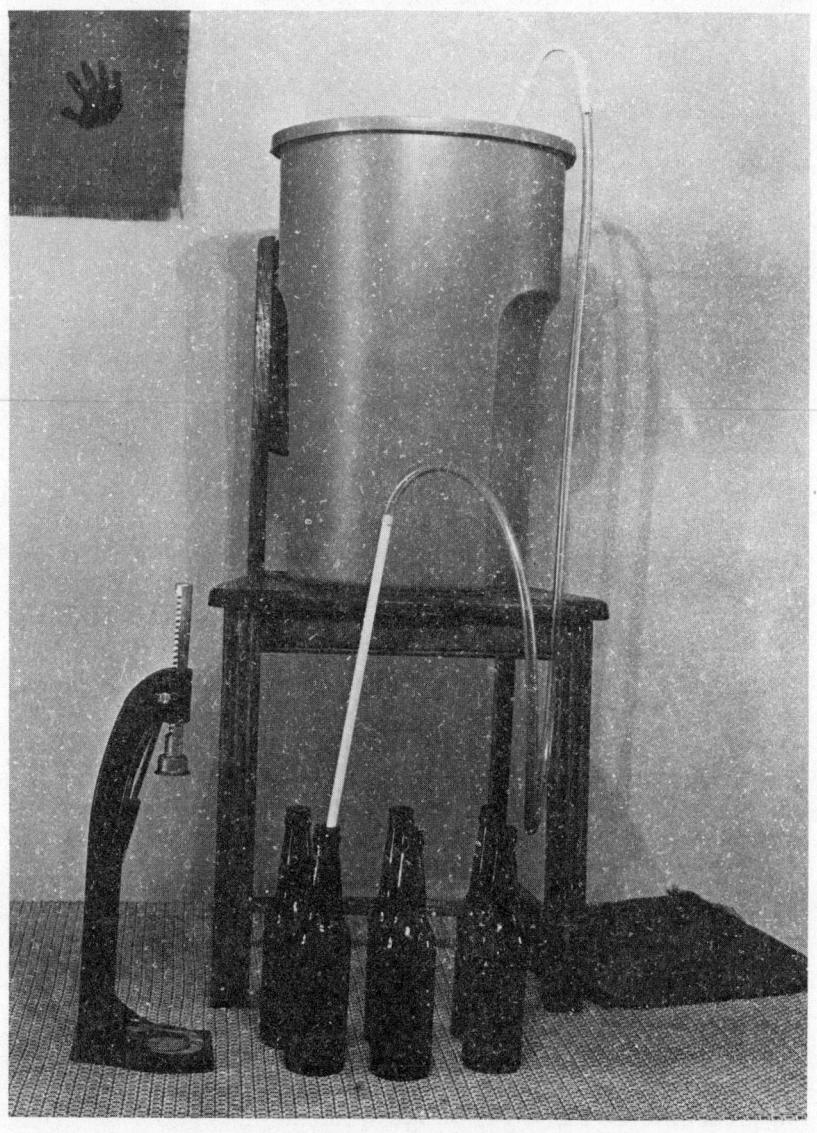

Equipment set up for bottling.

Siphoning primed beer into bottles, using the bottle filler, from a secondary fermenter.

AGING

While you can sample home brew after two weeks, longer aging is required for the best flavor. Ales and lagers should both be stored at fermentation temperature, or perhaps five degrees cooler if possible. Ales are fully mature after a month; lagers continue to improve for two to three months. I have known well hopped lager to survive a summer of storage at an average temperature of 75°F, but cannot recommend this. In any case six months is a conservative maximum for storing home brew.

You should label every bottle, since it can be very difficult to tell the contents otherwise. Some time after "putting down" a batch, I mark each bottle cap with a simple letter-number code. The letter tells the type of beer, and the number tells the batch. L3, for example, is my third batch of light lager. My code is: L = light lager; P = Pilsner; D = Dortmunder; M = Muenchner; E = Einbeck (Bock); A = Pale Ale; B = Bitter; N = Brown Ale; R = Porter; S = Stout. If I try another type of beer, I will have to assign it another letter.

I have one piece of advice on storing empty bottles: turn the cases upside down. That way waterbugs cannot get into the bottles.

SERVING

The basic pouring method has already been described. Once you get the hang of it, you will be able to control the depth of the head by regulating how much beer you pour down the side and how much into the middle. One problem which may puzzle you is a rapidly-collapsing head. This is usually caused by grease or detergent residue in your glass. After washing, rinse your beer glasses out three times in hot water, and let them drain. Never put them in the dishwasher.

In selecting glasses, never try to pour a twelve-ounce bottle of beer into a twelve-ounce glass. Because of the head, you will only get nine or ten ounces of beer into it and waste the rest.

One subject which is much debated is the ideal serving temperature. Most beers are chilled in the refrigerator to around 40 degrees. This is acceptable for light lagers; full-bodied lagers should be served somewhat warmer, at 45 to 50 degrees if possible. Ales can be drunk even warmer than this – up to 55 degrees. The English do not drink warm beer; they drink it at cellar temperature, which is cool, but not cold, and their beer is brewed to taste best at that temperature.

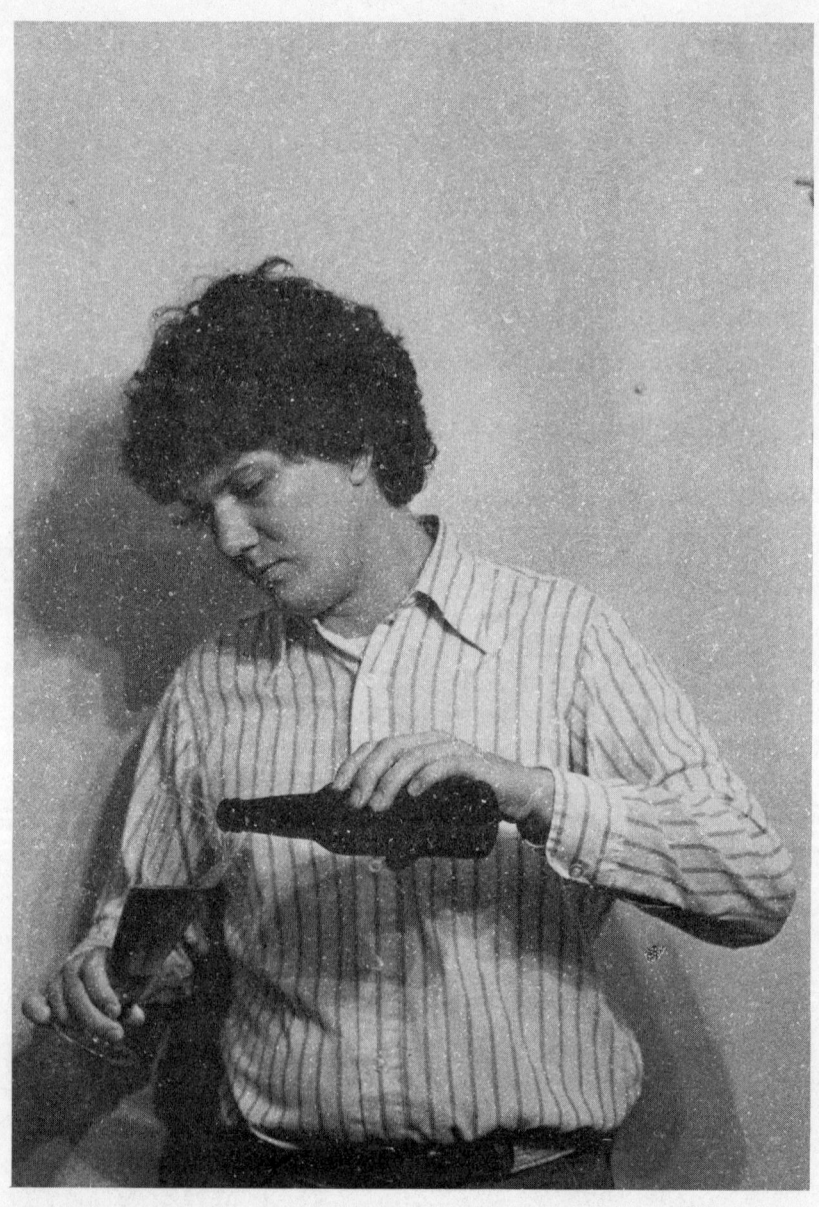

Proper technique for pouring beer into a glass. When glass is about half full, turn the glass straight up and pour the beer into the middle to get a good head.

Chapter 11

LAGERS

The following recipes all make use of the basic grain beer method described in the previous chapters. If you understand this method, you will have no trouble following these recipes.

Light lagers are light in both body and color; their low hop rate balances their lightness. I have given recipes for different types which vary significantly in flavor. I have not given recipes for many American beers because duplicating a commercial brand is virtually impossible. However, you can assess your own taste to try to determine what ingredients to use. For instance, if you favor Budweiser or Coor's, use rice rather than corn. Most other national brands (including Miller's, Schlitz, Pabst and Falstaff) use corn. The hop rate given should duplicate that of the milder beers. If you like a somewhat more bitter beer, try a slightly higher hop rate (around ¾ oz.). I personally favor Dutch and Scandinavian light lagers, which are more malty and have a better hop flavor than most American brands.

Pale lagers are pale in color, but not as pale as light lagers. They are full-bodied and malty, because no adjuncts are used in their brewing. German law prohibits the use of adjuncts and sugar in brewing. I give only two recipes, which cover the major types. Pilsner is brewed in many places besides Bohemia these days; however, most outlander Pilsners (including those brewed in Germany) use a lower hop rate than that of Pilsner Urquell. If you prefer a version less bitter than the original (and there is nothing wrong with that) lower the hop rate to 1½ ounces for five gallons.

Dark lagers are characterized by their color and the flavor of roasted malt. I give three recipes, which run the gamut from a fairly light-bodied brew to one of the strongest, most full-flavored lagers in existence. American Bock is light-bodied and mildly hopped; in fact, many commercial "bock beers" seem to be made by adding caramel coloring to the standard light lager. There are exceptions, however, and my recipe is modeled after the good bocks, such as the marvelous batch turned out by the Stag brewery in Belleville, Illinois during the winter of 1978–79. My recipe for Muenchner, on the other hand, cannot pretend to authenticity. Real Muenchner is made from special Munich malt, which is roasted darker than ordinary lager malt. This special malt is almost impossible to get, and so I have given an equivalent using roasted and caramel malts to approximate the color and flavor of the real thing. My personal preference in almost all dark beers, by the way, is for chocolate rather than black patent malt, but the flavors are different and you should try both. For Einbeck, the darkest of all lagers, the choice of roast malt will of course make more difference to the flavor. When serving this delicious brew – or Dortmunder, which is its pale equivalent – be sure to warn your guests that the alcohol content is around seven per cent, and so demands discretion on the part of the drinker!

DUTCH LIGHT LAGER – Starting Gravity 50

Ingredients

    9 gallons soft, neutral water (9 qts. mash + 5 gals. sparge, rest in reserve)
    6 lb. lager malt
    2 lb. rice
    1½ teaspoons or more Gypsum
    1 oz. Saaz or Cascade hops (boil)
    ¼ oz. same type hops (finishing)
    ¼ oz. same type hops (dry hops)
    1 teaspoon Irish Moss
    1 packet lager yeast
    ¼ cup Polyclar (optional)
    ½ teaspoon gelatine finings
    1 teaspoon Ascorbic acid
    1¼ cups corn sugar (priming)

Method

1. Grind the malt and prepare the brewing water. Wash the rice and boil in 6 quarts mash water until gelatinized (about 45 min.)

Add to remaining 3 quarts mash water, along with 1½ teaspoons Gypsum.
2. Bring mash water to 125°F and stir in malt. Protein rest 118–125°F for 45 minutes. Boost to 155°F in 20 minutes. Starch conversion rest 150–155°F for 20 minutes. Boost to 168°F and rest 5 minutes. During mash, check temperature and stir frequently. Always stir when applying heat.
3. Transfer mash to lauter tub, heat sparge water to 160°F and sparge.
4. Add more gypsum (if needed) to boiler and boil wort 1½ hours. After ½ hour add boiling hops; 15 minutes before end, add Irish Moss.
5. At end of boil, turn off heat, stir in finishing hops, and rest 1 hour.
6. Strain wort into primary, removing one quart for starter. Top up to 5 gallons if necessary, cover and force cool.
7. Meanwhile, force cool starter wort to 80°F and add yeast.
8. When wort is cool (70°F) stir up starter and pitch it in. Ferment in a cool place (50–55°F ideally). When fermentation slows down (SG approximately 17) put Polyclar and dry hops in bottom of secondary and rack. Fit airlock. After 2 days, add finings.
9. When fermentation is over (no gravity drop for 5 days) terminal gravity should be 11–13. Rack into primary, add ascorbic acid and priming sugar, and bottle. Age 2 to 3 months.

SCANDINAVIAN LIGHT LAGER – Starting Gravity 50

Ingredients

9 gallons soft, neutral water (9 qts. mash + 5 gals. sparge, rest in reserve)
6 lb. lager malt
2 lb. corn flakes or grits
1½ teaspoons or more Gypsum
1 oz. Hallertau or Tettnanger hops (boil)
¼ oz. same type hops (finishing)
¼ oz. same type hops (dry hops)
1 teaspoon Irish Moss

1 packet lager yeast
¼ cup Polyclar (optional)
½ teaspoon gelatine finings
1 teaspoon Ascorbic acid
1¼ cups priming sugar (corn sugar)

Method

1. Grind the malt and prepare the brewing water. Wash the grits (if used) and boil in 6 quarts mash water until gelatinized (about 40 min.). Add to remaining 3 quarts mash water along with 1½ teaspoons gypsum.
2. Bring mash water to 125°F and stir in malt (and cornflakes, if used). Protein rest 118–125°F for 45 minutes. Boost to 155°F in 20 minutes. Starch conversion rest 150–155°F for 20 minutes. Boost to 168°F and rest 5 minutes. During mash, check temperature and stir frequently. Always stir when applying heat.
3. Transfer mash to lauter tub, heat sparge water to 160°F, and sparge.
4. Add more gypsum (if needed) to boiler and boil wort 1½ hours. After ½ hour add boiling hops; 15 minutes before the end, add Irish Moss. At end of boil, turn off heat, stir in finishing hops, cover, and rest one hour.
5. Strain wort into primary and remove one quart for starter. Top up to 5 gallons if necessary, cover and force cool.
6. Meanwhile, force cool starter wort to 80°F and add yeast.
7. When wort is cooled to 70°F, stir up starter and pitch it in. Ferment cool (50–55°F ideally) until fermentation slows down (about SG 17). Put Polyclar and dry hops in bottom of secondary and rack. Fit airlock. After 2 days, add finings.
8. When fermentation is over (no gravity drop for 5 days) terminal gravity should be 11–13. Rack into primary, add ascorbic acid and priming sugar, and bottle. Age 2 to 3 months.

AMERICAN LIGHT LAGER – Starting Gravity 46

Ingredients
- 9 gallons soft, neutral water (9 qts. mash + 5 gals. sparge, rest in reserve)
- 5 lb. lager malt
- 2½ lb. rice *or* grits *or* cornflakes
- 1½ teaspoons or more Gypsum
- ⅔ oz. Cluster hops (boil)
- ⅓ oz. Cluster hops (finishing – optional)
- 1 teaspoon Irish Moss
- 1 packet lager yeast
- ¼ cup Polyclar (optional)
- ½ teaspoon gelatine finings
- 1 teaspoon ascorbic acid
- 1⅓ cups priming sugar (corn sugar)

Method
1. Prepare brewing water and grind the malt. Wash grits or rice (if used) and boil in 7½ quarts mash water until gelatinized (about 45 min.). Add to remaining 1½ qts. mash water along with 1½ teaspoons gypsum.
2. Bring mash water to 125°F and stir in malt (and cornflakes, if used). Protein rest 118–125°F for 45 minutes. Boost to 155°F in 25 minutes. Starch conversion rest 150–155°F for 20 minutes. Boost to 168°F and rest 5 minutes. During mash, check temperature and stir frequently. Always stir when applying heat.
3. Transfer mash to lauter tub, heat sparge water to 160°F, and sparge.
4. Add more gypsum (if needed) to boiler and boil 1½ hours. After ½ hour add boiling hops; 15 minutes before the end, add Irish Moss. At end of boil, turn off heat, stir in finishing hops (if used), cover, and rest for one hour.
5. Strain wort into primary and remove one quart for starter. Top up to 5 gallons if necessary, cover and force cool.
6. Meanwhile, force cool starter wort to 80°F and add yeast.

7. When wort is cool to 70°F, stir up starter and pitch it in. Ferment cool (50–55°F ideally) until fermentation slows down (about SG 17). Put Polyclar in bottom of secondary and rack. Fit airlock. After 2 days, add finings.
8. When fermentation is over (no gravity drop for 5 days) terminal gravity should be 10–12. Rack into primary, add ascorbic acid and priming sugar, and bottle. Age 2 months.

PILSNER STYLE PALE LAGER – Starting Gravity 48

Ingredients

    9 gallons soft, neutral water (8 qts. mash + 5 gals. sparge, rest in reserve)
    8 lbs. lager malt
    1½ teaspoons or more Gypsum
    2 oz. Saaz hops (boil)
    ½ oz. Saaz hops (finishing)
    ¼ oz. Saaz hops (dry hops)
    1 teaspoon Irish Moss
    1 packet lager yeast
    ¼ cup Polyclar (optional)
    ½ teaspoon gelatine finings
    1 teaspoon Ascorbic acid
    1¼ cups priming sugar (corn sugar)

Method

1. Prepare brewing water and grind the malt. Add 1½ teaspoons gypsum to the 8 qts. mash water.
2. Bring mash water to 125°F and stir in the malt. Protein rest 118–125°F for 45 minutes. Boost to 155°F in 15 minutes. Starch conversion rest 150–155°F for 20 minutes. Boost to 168°F and rest 5 minutes. During mash, check temperature and stir frequently. Always stir when applying heat.
3. Transfer mash to lauter tub, heat sparge water to 160°F, and sparge.
4. Add more gypsum (if needed) to boiler and boil 1½ hours. After ½ hour add boiling hops; 15 minutes before the end, add

Irish Moss. At end of boil, turn off heat, stir in finishing hops, cover, and rest one hour.
5. Strain wort into primary and remove one quart for starter. Top up to 5 gallons if necessary, cover and force cool.
6. Meanwhile, force cool starter wort to 80°F and add yeast.
7. When wort is cooled to 70°F, stir up starter and pitch it in. Ferment cool (50–55°F ideally) until fermentation slows down (about SG 17). Put Polyclar and dry hops in bottom of secondary and rack. Fit airlock. After 2 days, add finings.
8. When fermentation is over (no gravity drop for 5 days) terminal gravity should be around 12. Rack into primary, add ascorbic acid and priming sugar, and bottle. Age 2 to 3 months.

DORTMUNDER STYLE PALE LAGER – Starting Gravity 60

Ingredients

    9 gallons soft, neutral water (10 qts. mash + 6 gals. sparge, rest in reserve)
    9½ lbs. lager malt
    ½ lb. pale crystal malt
    1½ teaspoons or more Gypsum
    1½ oz. Saaz hops (boil)
    ¼ oz. Saaz hops (finishing)
    ¼ oz. Saaz hops (dry hops)
    1 teaspoon Irish Moss
    1 packet lager yeast
    ¼ cup Polyclar (optional)
    ½ teaspoon Gelatine finings
    1 teaspoon ascorbic acid
    1¼ cups priming sugar (corn sugar)

Method

1. Prepare brewing water and grind the malt (including crystal malt). Add 1½ teaspoons gypsum to the 10 qts. mash water.
2. Bring mash water to 125°F and stir in the malt. Protein rest 118–125°F for 45 minutes. Boost to 155°F in 20 minutes. Starch conversion rest 150–155°F for 25 minutes. Boost to 168°F and

rest 5 minutes. During mash, check temperature and stir frequently. Always stir when applying heat.
3. Transfer mash to lauter tub, heat sparge water to 160°F, and sparge.
4. Add more gypsum (if needed) to boiler and boil 1½ hours or more to reduce amount of wort to 5 gallons. After ½ hour add boiling hops; 15 minutes before the end, add Irish Moss. At end of boil, turn off heat, stir in finishing hops, cover, and rest one hour.
5. Strain wort into primary and remove one quart for starter. Top up to 5 gallons, if necessary, cover, and force cool.
6. Meanwhile, force cool starter wort to 80°F and add yeast.
7. When wort is cooled to 70°F, stir up starter and pitch it in. Ferment cool (50–55°F ideally) until fermentation slows down (about SG 18). Put Polyclar and dry hops in bottom of secondary and rack. Fit airlock. After 2 days, add finings.
8. When fermentation is over (no gravity drop for 5 days) terminal gravity should be around 13. Rack into primary, add ascorbic acid and priming sugar, and bottle. Age three months.

AMERICAN BOCK DARK LAGER – Starting Gravity 50

Ingredients

9 gallons soft, neutral water (9 qts. mash + 5 gals. sparge, rest in reserve)
6 lb. lager malt
2 oz. dark crystal malt
2 oz. black patent *or* 2½ oz. chocolate malt
2 lb. grits or cornflakes
1 oz. Hallertau or Tettnanger or ¾ oz. Cluster hops (boil)
¼ oz. same type hops (finishing)
1 teaspoon Irish Moss
1 packet lager yeast
¼ cup Polyclar (optional)
½ teaspoon gelatine finings
1 teaspoon ascorbic acid
1¼ cups priming sugar (corn sugar)

Method

1. Prepare brewing water and grind the malt, including dark malts. Wash the grits (if used) and boil in 6 qts. mash water until gelatinized (about 40 min.). Add to remaining 3 qts. mash water.
2. Bring the mash water to 125°F and stir in the malt (and cornflakes, if used). Protein rest 118–125°F for 45 minutes. Boost to 155°F in 20 minutes. Starch conversion rest 150–155°F for 25 minutes. Boost to 168°F and rest 5 minutes. During mash, check temperature and stir frequently. Always stir when applying heat.
3. Transfer mash to lauter tub, heat sparge water to 160°F, and sparge.
4. Boil for 1½ hours. After ½ hour add boiling hops; 15 minutes before the end, add Irish Moss. At end of boil, turn off heat, stir in finishing hops, cover, and rest one hour.
5. Strain wort into primary and remove one quart for starter. Top up to 5 gallons, if necessary, cover, and force cool.
6. Meanwhile, force cool starter wort to 80°F and add yeast.
7. When wort is cooled to 70°F, stir up starter and pitch it in. Ferment cool (50–55°F ideally) until fermentation slows down (about SG 17). Put Polyclar in bottom of secondary and rack. Fit airlock. After 2 days, add finings.
8. When fermentation is over (no gravity drop for 5 days) terminal gravity should be around 12. Rack into primary, add ascorbic acid and priming sugar, and bottle. Age two months.

MUENCHNER STYLE DARK LAGER – Starting Gravity 49

Ingredients

9 gallons soft, neutral water (8 qts. mash + 5 gals. sparge, rest in reserve)
8 lb. lager malt
2 oz. dark crystal malt
2 oz. black patent *or* 2½ oz. chocolate malt
1¼ oz. Hallertau hops (boil)
¼ oz. Hallertau hops (finishing)

¼ oz. Hallertau hops (dry hops)
1 teaspoon Irish Moss
1 packet lager yeast
¼ cup Polyclar (optional)
½ teaspoon gelatine finings
1 teaspoon ascorbic acid
1¼ cups priming sugar (corn sugar)

Method

1. Prepare the brewing water and grind all the malts.
2. Bring the mash water to 125°F and stir in the malt. Protein rest 118–125°F for 45 minutes. Boost to 155°F in 20 minutes. Starch conversion rest 150–155°F for 20 minutes. Boost to 168°F and rest 5 minutes. During mash, check temperature and stir frequently. Always stir when applying heat.
3. Transfer mash to lauter tub, heat sparge water to 160°F, and sparge.
4. Boil for 1½ hours. After ½ hour add boiling hops; 15 minutes before the end, add the Irish Moss. At end of boil, turn off heat, stir in finishing hops, cover, and rest one hour.
5. Strain wort into primary and remove one quart for starter. Top up to 5 gallons, if necessary; cover and force cool.
6. Meanwhile, force cool starter wort to 80°F and add yeast.
7. When wort is cooled to 70°F, stir up starter and pitch it in. Ferment cool (50–55°F ideally) until fermentation slows down (about SG 17). Put Polyclar and dry hops in bottom of secondary and rack. Fit airlock. After 2 days, add finings.
8. When fermentation is over (no gravity drop for 5 days) terminal gravity should be around 12. Rack into primary, add ascorbic acid and priming sugar, and bottle. Age two to three months.

EINBECK STYLE DARK LAGER – Starting Gravity 64

Ingredients

9 gallons soft, neutral water (10 qts. mash + 6 gals. sparge, rest in reserve)
10 lb. lager malt

4 oz. dark crystal malt
3½ oz. black patent *or* 5 oz. chocolate malt
1½ oz. Hallertau or Tettnanger hops (boil)
¼ oz. same type hops (finishing)
¼ oz. same type hops (dry hops)
1 teaspoon Irish Moss
1 packet lager yeast
¼ cup Polyclar (optional)
½ teaspoon gelatine finings
1 teaspoon ascorbic acid
1¼ cups priming sugar (corn sugar)

Method

1. Prepare the brewing water and grind all the malts.
2. Bring the mash water to 125°F and stir in the malt. Protein rest 118–125°F for 45 minutes. Boost to 155°F in 25 minutes. Starch conversion 150–155°F for 30 minutes. Boost to 168°F and rest 5 minutes. During mash, check temperature and stir frequently. Always stir when applying heat.
3. Transfer mash to lauter tub, heat sparge water to 160°F, and sparge.
4. Boil for 1½ hours, or more, if needed, to reduce volume of wort to 5 gallons. After ½ hour add boiling hops; 15 minutes before the end, add Irish Moss. At the end of the boil, turn off heat, stir in finishing hops, cover, and rest one hour.
5. Strain wort into primary and remove one quart for starter. Top up to 5 gallons, if necessary; cover and force cool.
6. Meanwhile, force cool starter wort to 80°F and add yeast.
7. When wort is cooled to 70°F, stir up starter and pitch it in. Ferment cool (50–55°F ideally) until fermentation slows down (about SG 20). Put Polyclar and dry hops in bottom of secondary, and rack. Fit airlock. After 2 days, add finings.
8. When fermentation is over (no gravity drop for 5 days) terminal gravity should be around 15. Rack into primary, add ascorbic acid and priming sugar, and bottle. Age three months or longer.

Chapter 12

ALES

Included in this chapter are a number of types of beer which are traditionally top-fermented. As with the recipes in the previous chapter, all these are based on the brewing method outlined in earlier chapters. I have adapted these recipes for lager malt, which is the only type widely available in the United States.

The chief adaptation – apart from the multi-temperature mash – is the use of a small amount of roast barley in the pale ale and bitter recipes. This is to compensate for the fact that lager malt is less roasted than British pale malt, and gives a lighter colored brew. In fact, pale ale is often copper or amber in hue, and pale only by comparison with the much darker brown ales and stouts produced in the United Kingdom.

Pale ale is characterized not only by its color, but its unique flavor as well. It is drier (lower terminal gravity) than lagers, but with a full complement of hop flavor and aroma. To get the low terminal gravity, I have specified a pound of corn sugar; however, a purist could substitute a pound of rice and lengthen the boost and starch conversion stages of the mash, which would get the same result – namely, increasing the percentage of fermentable sugar in the wort.

Bitter ale is often similar in color to pale ale, but is sweeter, with a higher terminal gravity. It is usually served on draught in Great Britain, but works equally well as a bottled beer for home brewers.

Brown ale is dark and sweet, with a low hop rate which lets the flavor of the roasted and crystal malts come through. In England it is often brewed with brown sugar, and if you wish, you may substitute one pound of dark brown sugar for one and a half pounds of malt. I prefer all-grain beers, but I must say that many ale experts disagree: why not try both recipes, and decide for yourself?

Porter and *stout* are both dry, smooth, bitter beers which were very popular in the nineteenth century. Porter, which is a lighter flavored brew, is now almost extinct commercially. Stout is represented chiefly by one famous Irish brand. Both use a generous amount of hops. In both recipes, roast barley is the first choice for the dark grain; fortunately, it is now available in this country. Please note that the brewing method is not identical to that given in the other recipes. I have found that the large amount of roast malt or barley can cause trouble with starch conversion if the entire amount is mashed with the pale malt. The method given avoids this problem, yet by adding the bulk of the roast grain before sparging, its full goodness can be extracted into the wort. The resulting brews will make you wonder about the current craze for lighter and lighter beers: it seems more sensible to drink one bottle of good porter than two or three gassy, tasteless "ultra-lights"!

PALE ALE – Starting Gravity 48

Ingredients

    9 gallons soft, neutral water (7 qts. mash + 5 gals. sparge, rest in reserve)
    1 lb. corn sugar
    7 lb. lager malt
    1 oz. dark crystal malt
    ½ oz. roast barley *or* black patent malt
    1½ teaspoons or more Gypsum
    1½ oz. Golding *or* ¾ oz. Fuggle *or* 1¼ oz. Northern Brewer or Brewer's Gold hops (boil)
    ½ oz. same type hops (finishing)
    ¼ oz. same type hops (dry hops)
    1 teaspoon Irish Moss
    1 packet ale yeast
    ¼ cup Polyclar (optional)
    1 teaspoon gelatine finings
    1 teaspoon Ascorbic acid
    1¼ cups priming sugar (corn sugar)

Method

1. Prepare the brewing water and grind the malts. Add 1½ teaspoons gypsum to the 7 qts. mash water.

2. Bring mash water to 125°F and stir in the malt. Protein rest 118–125°F for 45 minutes. Boost to 155°F in 40 minutes. Starch conversion rest 150–155°F for 45 minutes. Boost to 168°F and hold 5 minutes. During mash, check temperature and stir frequently. Always stir when applying heat.
3. Transfer mash to lauter tub, heat sparge water to 160°F, and sparge.
4. Add more gypsum (if needed) and the 1 lb. of corn sugar to the boiler and boil 1½ hours. After ½ hour add boiling hops; 15 minutes before the end, add Irish Moss. At end of boil, turn off heat, stir in finishing hops, cover, and rest one hour.
5. Strain wort into primary and remove one quart for starter. Top up to 5 gallons if necessary, cover and force cool.
6. Meanwhile, force cool starter wort to 90°F and add yeast.
7. When wort is cooled to 70°F, stir up starter and pitch it in. Ferment at low room temperature (60–65°F ideally) until fermentation slows down (about SG 14). Put Polyclar and dry hops in bottom of secondary and rack. Fit airlock. After 2 days, add finings.
8. When fermentation is over (no gravity drop for 5 days) terminal gravity should be around 9. Rack into primary, add ascorbic acid and priming sugar, and bottle. Age one month.

BITTER ALE – Starting Gravity 50

Ingredients

9 gallons soft, neutral water (8½ qts. mash + 5 gals. sparge, rest in reserve)
8 lb. lager malt
½ lb. dark crystal malt
½ oz. roast barley *or* black patent malt
1½ teaspoons or more Gypsum
1½ oz. Golding *or* ¾ oz. Fuggle *or* 1¼ oz. Northern Brewer or Brewer's Gold hops (boil)
¼ oz. same type hops (finishing)
¼ oz. same type hops (dry hops)
1 teaspoon Irish Moss
1 packet ale yeast

¼ cup Polyclar (optional)
1 teaspoon gelatine finings
1 teaspoon ascorbic acid
1¼ cups priming sugar (corn sugar)

Method

1. Prepare the brewing water and grind the malts. Add 1½ teaspoons gypsum to the 8½ qts. mash water.
2. Bring the mash water to 125°F and stir in the malt. Protein rest 118–125°F for 45 minutes. Boost to 155°F in 45 minutes. Starch conversion rest 150–155°F for 45 minutes. Boost to 168°F and rest 5 minutes. During mash, check temperature and stir frequently. Always stir when applying heat.
3. Transfer mash to lauter tub, heat sparge water to 160°F, and sparge.
4. Add more gypsum (if needed) to the boiler and boil 1½ hours. After ½ hour add the boiling hops; 15 minutes before the end, add Irish Moss. At end of boil, turn off heat, stir in the finishing hops, cover, and rest one hour.
5. Strain wort into primary and remove one quart for starter. Top up to 5 gals. if necessary, cover and force cool.
6. Meanwhile, force cool starter wort to 90°F and add yeast.
7. When wort is cooled to 70°F, stir up starter and pitch it in. Ferment at low room temperature (60–65°F ideally) until fermentation slows down (about SG 17). Put Polyclar and dry hops in bottom of secondary and rack. Fit airlock. After 2 days, add finings.
8. When fermentation is over (no gravity drop for 5 days) terminal gravity should be around 12. Rack into primary, add ascorbic acid and priming sugar, and bottle. Age one month.

BROWN ALE – Starting Gravity 52

Ingredients

9 gallons soft, neutral water (9 qts. mash + 5½ gals. sparge, rest in reserve)
8 lb. lager malt

½ lb. dark crystal malt
4 oz. chocolate malt *or* 3 oz. black patent malt
1 oz. Northern Brewer or Brewer's Gold hops (boil)
¼ oz. same type hops (finishing)
1 teaspoon Irish Moss
1 packet ale yeast
¼ cup Polyclar (optional)
1 teaspoon gelatine finings
1 teaspoon ascorbic acid
1⅛ cups priming sugar (corn sugar)

Method

1. Prepare brewing water and grind the malts.
2. Bring the mash water to 125°F and stir in the malt. Protein rest 118–125°F for 45 minutes. Boost to 155°F in 40 minutes. Starch conversion rest 150–155°F for 40 minutes. Boost to 168°F and rest 5 minutes. During mash, check temperature and stir frequently. Always stir when applying heat.
3. Transfer mash to lauter tub, heat sparge water to 160°F, and sparge.
4. Boil 1½ hours. After ½ hour, add the boiling hops; 15 minutes before the end, add Irish Moss. At end of boil, turn off heat, stir in the finishing hops, cover, and rest one hour.
5. Strain wort into primary and remove one quart for starter. Top up to 5 gallons, if necessary; cover and force cool.
6. Meanwhile, force cool starter wort to 90°F and add yeast.
7. When wort is cooled to 70°F, stir up starter and pitch it in. Ferment at low room temperature (60–65°F ideally) until fermentation slows down (about SG 19). Put Polyclar in bottom of secondary and rack. Fit airlock. After 2 days, add finings.
8. When fermentation is over (no gravity drop for 5 days) terminal gravity should be around 14. Rack into primary, add ascorbic acid and priming sugar, and bottle. Age one month.

PORTER – Starting Gravity 50

Ingredients

9 gallons soft, neutral water (8½ qts. mash + 5 gals. sparge, rest in reserve)
8 lb. lager malt
7 oz. roast barley *or* 8 oz. chocolate malt *or* 6 oz. black patent malt
1½ oz. Northern Brewer or Brewer's Gold hops (boil)
¼ oz. same type hops (finishing – optional)
1 packet ale yeast
¼ cup Polyclar (optional)
1 teaspoon gelatine finings
1 teaspoon ascorbic acid
1 cup priming sugar (corn sugar)

Method

1. Prepare the brewing water. Grind 2½ oz. roast barley or dark malt together with the pale lager malt. Grind the remaining dark malt *separately* and put in a small saucepan. Add enough water to make a thick porridge, and simmer this roast malt mixture over very low heat during the mash.
2. Bring the mash water to 125°F and stir in the lager malt plus 2½ oz. of the dark grain. Protein rest 118–125°F for 30 minutes. Boost to 155°F in 50 minutes. Starch conversion rest 150–155°F for 45 minutes. At end of starch conversion rest, stir in the dark grain porridge and rest 5 minutes. DO NOT BOOST to 168°F.
3. Transfer mash to lauter tub, heat sparge water to 160°F, and sparge.
4. Boil 1 hour. As soon as wort comes to a boil, add boiling hops. At end of boil, turn off heat, stir in finishing hops, cover, and rest 1 hour.
5. Strain wort into primary and remove one quart for starter. Top up to 5 gallons, if necessary; cover and force cool.
6. Meanwhile, force cool starter wort to 90°F and add yeast.
7. When wort is cooled to 70°F, stir up starter and pitch it in. Ferment at low room temperature (60–65°F ideally) until

fermentation slows down (about SG 14). Put Polyclar in bottom of secondary and rack. Fit airlock. After 2 days, add finings.
8. When fermentation is over (no gravity drop for 5 days) terminal gravity should be around 9. Rack into primary, add ascorbic acid and priming sugar, and bottle. Age one month.

STOUT – Starting Gravity 60

Ingredients

    9 gallons soft, neutral water (10 qts. mash + 6 gals. sparge, rest in reserve)
    8 lb. lager malt
    14 oz. roast barley *or* 1 lb. chocolate malt *or* 12 oz. black patent malt
    1 lb. barley or barley flakes
    2 oz. Northern Brewer or Brewer's Gold hops (boil)
    1 packet ale yeast
    ¼ cup Polyclar (optional)
    1 teaspoon gelatine finings
    1 teaspoon ascorbic acid
    1 cup priming sugar (corn sugar)

Method

1. Prepare the brewing water. Grind 2½ oz. roast barley or dark malt together with the pale lager malt. Grind the remaining dark grain separately and put in a small saucepan. Add enough water to make a thick porridge, and simmer this roast malt mixture over very low heat during the mash. Boil the barley (if used) in 3 qts. mash water until gelatinized (about 1½ hours). Add to remaining 7 quarts mash water.
2. Bring the mash water to 125°F and stir in the lager malt plus 2½ oz. of the dark grain. Protein rest 118–125°F for 30 minutes. Boost to 155°F in 50 minutes. Starch conversion rest 150–155°F for 50 minutes. At end of starch conversion rest, stir in the dark grain porridge and rest 5 minutes. DO NOT BOOST to 168°F.
3. Transfer mash to lauter tub, heat sparge water to 160°F, and sparge.

4. Boil one hour or longer, if necessary, to reduce volume of wort to 5 gallons. As soon as wort comes to a boil, add hops. At end of boil, turn off heat, cover, and rest one hour.
5. Strain wort into primary and remove one quart for starter. Top up to 5 gallons, if necessary; cover and force cool.
6. Meanwhile, force cool starter wort to 90°F and add yeast.
7. When wort is cooled to 70°F, stir up starter and pitch it in. Ferment at low room temperature (60–65°F ideally) until fermentation slows down (about SG 17). Put Polyclar in bottom of secondary and rack. Fit airlock. After 2 days, add finings.
8. When fermentation is over (no gravity drop for 5 days) terminal gravity should be around 12. Rack into primary, add ascorbic acid and priming sugar, and bottle. Age one month.

Chapter 13

PROBLEMS

I. INFECTIONS

Many sorts of bacteria and wild yeasts can infect beer. Acetic and lactic acid bacteria are the most common.

The obvious symptom of acetic bacteria is a vinegary smell and taste in the beer. Lactic acid will give a sour taste and "ropey" consistency. Wild yeasts are sometimes responsible for persistent hazes (*not* chill haze). In all cases, there is no cure. You must throw out the infected beer and start over.

This grim prospect should motivate you to practice preventive medicine. Sterilize everything that touches your beer; but remember that chlorine kills yeast, and rinse equipment thoroughly to remove all traces of chlorine after sterilizing.

Apart from sterilization, prevention is basically good brewing practice. Keep the bitter wort covered during cooling, and when it is cool, pitch it with a working starter that will take hold and squeeze out competing organisms.

It is equally important to keep the beer away from air during secondary fermentation. Most infections are airborne, and even well-hopped beer will eventually turn to vinegar if left in contact with air at room temperature.

If you must skimp on cleaning, do so with equipment used *before* boiling, since boiling sterilizes the wort. One piece of equipment that should not be exposed to chlorine detergent is the grain bag, because it is very hard to rinse the cleaning agent out of the canvas. Plenty of hot water will do the job. But for everything past the boiling stage, sterilization must be strictly observed.

II. HAZE

The most common, if not the most serious, defect in home brewed beer is haze. Sometimes a beer will throw a haze at storage temperatures, but far more common is chill haze, which appears when the beer is cooled before drinking. The reaction can be reversed: as the beer warms up, the haze will disappear.

Before trying Polyclar, I made a long investigation of the haze problem, and hope to publish some of my research some day. But from a practical point of view, all the home brewer really needs to know is that treatment in the secondary with a quarter cup of Polyclar, as described in Chapter Nine, will chillproof even the heaviest all-malt lagers, provided only that the mash has included a 45 minute protein rest. I would add that I recommend Polyclar even for beers too dark to show a haze, because it also removes certain products of oxidation which can harm the flavor of even a dark beer. Home brew tends to be heavily oxidized because of our equipment limitations. In fact, haze and oxidation are closely related, and – well, I urge you to try Polyclar.

III. TASTE

Some problems with the taste of beer are the result of misunderstanding; others of accident or oversight. I have tried to list all common complaints and some possible causes. Here is where your log will really help you.

1. *Salty.* There is only one remedy: do not use salt (table salt, sodium chloride) in beer. Ignore recipes which say otherwise.

2. *Thin* (Lack of body). Most extract beers are made from half extract and half corn sugar. They lack the "palate fulness" of an all-grain beer. Diet beers are also thin, and for the same reason: to cut down the calories, you have to cut down the amount of grain.

3. *Too Dry* (lack of sweetness or malty flavor). This may be the result of the recipe: see the comments under (2) above. The basic symptom is a low terminal gravity, and for a grain beer, the cure is to adjust your mash procedure to get more dextrins in the wort. (See Chapter 7.)

4. *Too Sweet.* The cure is as above, only in reverse. Alter your mash technique to get a *lower* proportion of dextrins in the wort.

5. *Sour.* This could be due to an infection: see Section I in this Chapter. You may also have used a recipe calling (as many do) for the addition of a full teaspoon of pure powdered citric acid to your extract wort. This is about eight times more acid than is needed to neutralize nine gallons of lime-treated, highly alkaline city water, and is enough to give the beer a taste faintly reminiscent of Kool-Aid. Next time leave it out.

6. *Too Bitter.* This complaint can have many causes, and you should refer to your log to help you form hypotheses and track down the cause.

One cause is failure to skim the bitter crud off the head during primary fermentation. The cure is obvious.

Another cause is a defective cold break, caused by slow cooling. Always force cool your wort.

Immature beers will still contain bitter tasting yeast in suspension, even though they may look clear. This "yeasty" bitterness found in "green" beer is different from the harshness caused by real mistakes, and you should have no trouble telling the difference.

You may have used a bad recipe which called for more hops than are traditionally used for the type of beer you made. Check your recipe against my recommendations.

A related problem is substituting a different type of hop with a higher bittering power. See the section on hops in Chapter Four for a discussion of hop rates.

I have occasionally gotten a mislabeled package of hops. It is not easy for an inexperienced brewer to tell one kind of hop from another by sight or smell, and you should try to find reliable sources for your brewing ingredients.

Never trust the stated weight on a hop package. "Guesstimations" and overweight packages can lead to overhopped beers. Buy a scale.

Bad brewing water can cause harsh bitterness. The more sodium and/or magnesium there is in your water supply, the lower your hop rates will have to be.

Finally, it must be stated that bitterness is a matter of what you are used to. Compare your home brew with a commercially made, imported brand of the same type. If the bitterness is comparable, you have probably done nothing wrong. American beers are among the least hopped in the world, partly, I suspect, because of the harshness of American hops. But it takes some time to adjust to the stronger flavor of European beers.

7. *Flat.* If the entire batch is really flat, with no fizz at all, you probably forgot to add priming syrup to the batch at bottling time. Another possibility is that the bottles were not adequately rinsed after sterilizing with chlorine, and the yeast was killed.

Unless your beer was in the secondary for several months, it is *very* unlikely that there was not enough yeast in the beer to cause the bottle fermentation. You can safely dismiss this possibility.

If only one bottle is flat, it was improperly capped or chipped at the mouth, and the carbon dioxide escaped.

If the beer is undercarbonated, increase the amount of priming sugar next time you bottle. My priming rates reflect those used commercially for the same type of beer. Again, American beer is highly carbonated, which matches the low temperatures at which it is drunk. Full flavored beers, intended for drinking at higher temperatures, need less carbonation; if they are served cold, they may seem flat.

8. *Overcarbonation.* This can be a headache, making serving very difficult. You may have used too much priming sugar. You may also have used cane sugar rather than corn sugar. This can be done, but you must use the table of equivalents. Cup-for-cup substitution will give almost twice as much carbonation as called for.

9. *No Head.* Naturally carbonated beers usually produce a fine head. The first thing to check is carbonation. If the beer is well carbonated, there are several possible explanations.

First, your serving glass may be contaminated with grease or detergent. Pour a fresh beer into a clean glass, washed rinsed and dried as specified in Chapter Ten.

Second, extract beers and low malt beers do not contain much head-forming protein, and may need the help of a heading compound.

Dark beers also tend to have less head retention than pale beers, and may benefit from heading compound and a shorter protein rest.

Finally, a warm fermentation will result in a massive amount of foam. If the head is skimmed often, most of that foam – along with the heading protein it contains – will be eliminated from the finished beer, and there may not be enough protein left to produce a good head. Try to remove only contaminated parts of the head, and if your ale is fermented at over 65°F, consider heading compound as an insurance policy.

IV. PROCEDURE

I have tried to mention and suggest remedies for most procedural problems as they come up in the brewing process. Here I want to urge readers to use their own common sense and ingenuity to augment my advice. For instance, you may have to adjust for limited equipment. Until I bought my eight-gallon boiler, I boiled my wort in two shifts in the mash kettle. This is time-consuming, but it works.

Another example: the cheap faucet on my lauter tub is not big enough for the job. It works, but it will only pass pieces of grain husks when it is wide open. Because of the fast flow, I *always* get a set mash, and use the set mash procedure described in Chapter Seven. I do not waste time trying to run the wort off slowly. I have found that if the procedure is carefully followed, you can get a flow of sparge water just as fast as through a properly drained, un-set grain mass, and the wort is just as clear.

I hope that these examples will encourage you to be creative in coping with the limitations imposed by your equipment. Try my methods first, to save yourself all of my mistakes; but then try to improve on them. Chances are you will be able to.

V. IMAGINARY PROBLEMS

At least two of these deserve comment. The first is starch conversion. American malt is so loaded with diastase that starch conversion is almost automatic, even if pH and temperature are not exactly right. For this reason I have not mentioned, and do not recommend, an iodine test to see if starch conversion is complete.

The iodine will react to grain husks just as well as to grain starch, and will give a color change if there are any finely ground pieces of grain husk in the sample tested. I know one brewer with some very fine-ground malt who kept a mash going for a week, trying to get a negative reading on the iodine test! Instead, use your index finger. By tasting the mash every five minutes, you will find that after about fifteen minutes in the high-temperature rest the mash is not getting any sweeter. This means the starch is all converted. Do not stop the rest at this point, however – more time is needed to break down more of the dextrins into maltose.

The second imaginary problem is non-starting and "stuck" fermentations. Nobody I know of has ever had either. If you make a starter at the right temperature (excessive heat *will* kill yeast), and add energizer to get a quicker start, the beer will soon begin to ferment. Remember that, like boilovers, lag period jitters are just part of learning the craft.

Chapter 14

THE BREWER'S CALENDAR

Home brewing requires more planning than most other hobbies. If you intend to make all or most of the beer you drink, you will need to think about the supplies you will need to produce the required amount of brew. The time to begin planning is before the brewing season starts.

I use the term "brewing season" to refer to the six months of the year when most of the nation is cold enough to make home brewing an enjoyable activity. In warm weather, kitchens are hot – especially with beer on the stove – and the outdoors beckons. By careful planning you can probably turn out enough beer in six months to last you the other half of the year.

The first consideration is how much you drink. If you can make a realistic estimate of this, you can easily calculate the number of brewing sessions you will need to have during the winter.

I prefer to buy all my ingredients for an entire season at one shot. So I sit down with my notebook and make out a tentative schedule, with all the recipes I intend to try, and the dates for each session. I try to make my lager during the coldest months, when my basement is cool enough for proper fermentation. I make ales in the fall and spring.

Once I have planned out a brewing season in this way, I make a tally sheet and go through each recipe, keeping a running total of all the ingredients I will need. Then I go back over the list to make sure I have not forgotten something. It is easy to overlook small, peripheral items like bottle caps – but just try to make beer without them!

Ordering everything in advance assures that you will have what you need, when you need it. It is easy to waste valuable time in repeated trips to the local winemakers' store for one or two small items. You also run the risk of not being able to find what you want. As the hobby grows, home brewing supplies will be easier to get, but as of now, even the best stocked retailers have occasional problems with keeping some items in stock. You will probably find that no one retailer – local or mail-order – carries everything you need. I urge you to send for catalogs from the suppliers listed in Appendix C, and any others you can find.

Planning is the key to saving time in a single brewing session, just as it is for the whole season. If you follow my suggestions, you will soon be able to make an all-grain wort in two to three hours, which is a worthwhile trade-off of time for beer quality. Here I want to suggest a few additional time-saving measures. Chances are that you will not be able to use all of them, but one or two may help.

If your water must be boiled, do this the night before, and let the water cool (covered) overnight. You will have to use your boiler and mash kettle together to get the required nine gallons of soft, neutral water; cover the vessels to minimize boiloff, and start with ten gallons to be sure you will end up with enough water.

If your water is lime-treated and must be neutralized, the following trick can save you a lot of time. The first time you brew, draw your nine gallons of water from your *hot* water tap. Neutralize it, and note the amount of acid required. If you divide this amount by nine, you will have the amount required to neutralize one gallon of water, and you will not need to collect and treat all your brewing water in advance. But the major advantage is that you will be able to take advantage of your home water heater and greatly reduce the amount of time you spend waiting for water to warm up. You can draw your mash water straight into the mash kettle and neutralize it, then (for pale beers) add the gypsum; it will probably need very little heating to achieve the proper "mash-in" temperature of 125°F. The same principle applies to sparging. Sparge water will need only a few minutes to bring it up to 160°F if you can take it from the hot water tap and neutralize it in the kettle.

I have already suggested collecting the last couple of gallons of sweet wort in a separate vessel while you are bringing the first fraction to a boil. An even better idea, if you can arrange it, is to place your lauter tub over the stove, so that you can be heating the wort while it is running into the boiler. Just remember that the boiling time does not begin until all the wort is kicking and rolling.

Once again let me repeat that planning is vital to your success as a home brewer. With planning and a little ingenuity, you will soon find beermaking no more complicated than most other forms of cooking. You will wonder that you ever found mashing mysterious or frightening. You will also feel the satisfaction that comes when you put your feet up and enjoy a glass of beer so smooth and mellow that your friends swear "it doesn't taste like home brew at all!"

Appendix A

AN OUTLINE OF HOME BREWING

I. **Malting**
   This is done by professionals. The Amateur buys his malt from a retailer.

II. **Making Sweet Wort**
   A. Grinding – Malt is ground in a hand mill.
   B. Water Treatment – Water is either boiled or neutralized to produce "soft, neutral water". Water is then hardened with gypsum if necessary.
   C. Cooking Cereal – If recipe calls for adjuncts, these grains may be purchased as flakes which are ready for mashing. Otherwise the cereal – rice, corn grits, or barley – must be boiled in the mash water.
   D. Mash – Ground malt is mixed with mash water and adjuncts at 125°F.
      1. Protein rest – 30–45 minutes at 122°F.
      2. Boost – to 155°F in 15–30 minutes.
      3. Starch Conversion rest – 20–30 minutes at 152°F.
      4. Boost to 168°F as fast as possible.
      5. Rest at 165°F for 5–10 minutes.
   E. Sparging – Mash is transferred to lauter tub, drained, and rinsed with 5–6 gallons of hot water.

III. **Making Bitter Wort**
   Wort is boiled for an hour or more with *hops*, which release their bitterness into the liquid.

IV. **Fermentation**
   A. Bitter wort is force-cooled.
   B. Bitter wort is pitched with a yeast starter.
   C. Primary fermentation – beer ferments rapidly in an open vessel.
   D. Racking – beer is siphoned to a closed container.
   E. Secondary fermentation – Beer ferments slowly in closed container.

V. Bottling and Aging
The beer, when fermented, is *primed* with a small amount of corn sugar and bottled. It is aged for one to three months before drinking.

Appendix B

BIBLIOGRAPHY

I list here a few books which I have found helpful. The last two are very expensive professional texts which you should get from a library before deciding to buy. Of the amateur books, Dave Line's are particularly good in their explanation of mashing theory and practice. Unfortunately – like all the amateur books – they are aimed at Britons using pale ale malt, which requires a very different mashing system from American lager malt. The hop rates are also different (see page 26).

Berry, C. J. J. *Home Brewed Beers and Stouts*, Amateur Winemaker Publications Ltd., Andover, Hants. 1963.
Line, Dave. *The Big Book of Brewing*, Amateur Winemaker Publications Ltd., 1974.
Line, Dave. *Brewing Beers Like Those You Buy*, Amateur Winemaker Publications Ltd., 1978.
Shales, Ken. *Brewing Better Beers*, Amateur Winemaker Publications Ltd., 1967.

---

de Clerck, Jean. *A Textbook of Brewing*, translated by K. Barton-Wright. London, Chapman-Hall Ltd., 1957.
Hough, Briggs, and Stevens. *Malting and Brewing Science*, Chapman-Hall Ltd., 1971.

Of these two books, de Clerck's is easier for non-chemists to understand and is less theoretical. The Hough volume is more up-to-date and contains more information on topics of interest to home brewers, such as hops and haze prevention. Try to borrow both if possible.

Appendix C

MAIL ORDER SOURCES

Wine and the People,
907 University Ave.,
Berkeley, CA 94710

E. C. Kraus,
P.O. Box 7850,
Independence, MO 64053

Semplex of U.S.A.,
Box 12276,
Minneapolis, Minnesota 55412

Bierhaus International Inc.,
2041 West 12th Street,
Erie PA 16505

Earl C. Martin, Western Winecraft,
336 Sudbury Avenue,
Penticton, B.C. V2A 3W5 Canada

New England Winemaking Supply,
501 Worcester Rd., Route 9,
Framingham, Mass.01701

Premier Malt Products Inc.,
1037 W. KcKinley Ave.,
Milwaukee WI 53201

Dover Vineyards,
24945 Detroit Rd.,
Westlake Ohio 44145

The Home Brew Company,
2328 Taraval Street,
San Francisco CA 94116

Bacchus and Barleycorn,
6110 Johnson Drive,
Mission, Kansas 66202

Winemakers Ltd.,
999 Main Rd., Box C.406,
Westport, Mass. 02790

Wines Inc.,
1340 Home Avenue,
Akron, Ohio 44310

Niagara Vine Products Ltd.,
P.O. Box 578, St. Catharines,
Ontario, Canada, L2R 6W8

Oregon Speciality Co.,
Portland, Oregon 97213

Indian Valley Farms Inc.,
RTE.1. Wapato, WA 98951

Ye Olde Wine Shoppe,
1135 W. Hildebrand Ave.,
San Antonio, Texas 78201

Great Fermentations,
87 Larkspur,
San Rafael, CA 94901

Winemakers House,
123 East William Street,
San Jose, CA 95112

Wine Art Sales Ltd.,
3429 West Broadway,
Vancouver, B.C. VCR 2B4

The Cellar,
10314 Main Street,
Fairfax, Virginia 22030

The Home Winemaking Shop,
22941 Ventura Blvd,
Woodlands Hills, CA 91364

The Malt Shop,
1018 W. Cummings St.,
Henryetta, OKLA 74437

Wine & Brew By You Inc.,
5760 Bird Road,
S. Miami, FLA 33155

The Winemakers Shop,
434 State Street,
Madison, WIS 53703

The Wine Works,
392 Waterloo Street,
London, Ontario N6B 2N8

Evelyn's Winemaking Supplies,
9220 N. 7th Street,
Phoenix, Arizona 85020

Lil Ole Winemakers Supply,
731 New Warrington Rd.,
Fensacola, FL 32506

Unique Inc.,
5319 W. 86th Street,
Indianapolis, Indiana 46268

Winemakers Ltd.,
11 Riverfield Drive,
Weston, CONN 06883

Woodcraft Supply Corp.,
313 Montvale Avenue,
Woburn, Mass 01801

Another source which must be mentioned is Wine-Art, a Canadian company with franchised dealerships in most major cities of the United States. Check your yellow pages to find the nearest outlet. All these companies have free catalogs which you should send for.

This list does not constitute a recommendation or endorsement, and I am sure that there are other, equally reputable mail-order retailers whom I am not familiar with. If you know, or hear of, businesses which are not listed here, by all means try them. A home brewer needs as many suppliers as possible.

Appendix D

EQUIVALENT WEIGHTS AND MEASURES

Here I give only a few equivalents for the British and American systems. I have ignored metrics because the system has yet to be adopted here, and looks to be a while in coming.

British *weights* are the same as American weights. British volumetric measures are as follows:

One U.S. gallon	= 0.833 Imperial gallons
One U.S. quart	= 0.833 Imperial quarts
One Imperial gallon	= 1.2 U.S. gallons

Other than these, most numbers for British recipes translate directly: but see the section on hop rates for an important exception!

If you understand the "degrees of extract" concept (see Chapter Eight), the following table will help you calculate substitutions. Remember, if you *must* substitute cane sugar, never, never do so cup for cup. Go by *weight*, and use $4/5$ the weight of cane sugar to get the same amount of alcohol or carbonation.

Ingredient	Yield (Degrees of Extract)	Volume
1 lb. corn sugar	40	2 $2/3$ cups
1 lb. cane sugar (white)	50	2 cups
1 lb. pale malt	30 (approx.)	varies
1 lb. crystal malt	15 (approx.)	varies
1 lb. British malt extract	45 (approx.)	n.a.
1 lb. American malt extract	39 (approx.)	n.a.
1 lb. Grain adjunct	35 (approx.)	n.a.

GLOSSARY

Acetic acid – the acid in vinegar; in beer, it is the result of infection by an airborne bacterium.
Acid – any sour-tasting chemical which reacts with alkalis to form salts; more technically, any compound which yields hydrogen ions in solution.
Adjuncts – unmalted cereal grains which can be mashed along with barley malt. They contribute extra starch which is converted, along with the malt starch, into sugar. Adjuncts must be cooked before mashing.
Alcohol – in brewing, always refers to ethyl alcohol, the kind that you can drink. A product of fermentation.
Ale – any beer brewed according to traditional English practices, and fermented with top-fermenting yeast.
Alkali – any bitter-tasting chemical which reacts with acids to form salts; more technically, any compound which yields hydroxyl (OH) ions in solution.
Alpha Acid – Humulon, the bitter resin responsible for most of the bitterness of the hop cone.
Alpha amylase – an enzyme produced by malting barley; it converts malt starch to dextrins during mashing.
Amylase – Alpha or beta amylase, or both.
Ascorbic acid – Vitamin C; used to prevent oxidation of beer.
Balling – another scale on the hydrometer, not used by home brewers. One degree Balling (or Brix, which is the same thing) equals about 3.8 points on the specific gravity scale.
Beta Acid – Lupulon, another bitter resin contained in the hop cone.
Beta Amylase – an enzyme produced by malting barley; it converts dextrins to maltose during mashing.
Bitter wort – Wort which has been made bitter by boiling with hops. See also *wort* and *sweet wort*.
Body – term used to describe the palate fulness of the finished beer. Full-bodied beers have a kind of rich, thick "feel" on the tongue.
Break – the clumping together of invisible protein molecules to form visible clumps in the wort.
Brix – see *Balling*.
Brewing – the art of turning barley, water, hops and yeast into beer; the term refers particularly to the mashing and boiling stages.
Calcium chloride – a water treatment salt which is very useful in the brewing of certain "hard water" beers.
Campden tablets – potassium metabisulfite, a source of sulfur dioxide.
Carbon dioxide – a tingly gas produced by fermentation; responsible for the fizz in beer.
Carbonation – the process of dissolving carbon dioxide gas in beer; usually accomplished in the bottle when making home brew.
Carboy – a large, narrow-necked glass bottle; useful as a secondary fermenter.

Catalyst – any chemical which greatly speeds up a chemical reaction (such as the conversion of starch to sugar) without being changed itself in the process. Enzymes are natural, organic catalysts.
Chalk – calcium carbonate, an alkaline salt sometimes used in brewing dark beers.
Citric acid – the predominate acid in many fruits; when used in beer, gives it a fruity flavor.
Corn sugar – glucose produced from corn starch; the best sugar for home brewing purposes.
Cubitainer – a five gallon semi-rigid plastic cube, useful as a secondary fermenter.
Dextrins – complex, unfermentable sugars produced from starch by the action of Alpha amylase during mashing; some dextrins remain in the finished beer and give it its malty sweetness.
Diastase – Alpha and beta amylase, taken together. It is sometimes useful to lump these two enzymes together for purposes of chemical analysis, and the name for this composite is diastase.
Dry – in describing the flavor of beer, dry is the opposite of sweet. Sweet beers are richer in dextrins (see *dextrins*) than dry beers, and have a higher specific gravity.
Enzyme – see *catalyst*.
Extract – (1) malt extract. (2) the sugar obtained, or extracted, from the malt grain during mashing.
Extraction – the process of removing or getting one thing from another; for example, getting malt sugars from malt.
Fermentation – the process in which yeast "feeds" upon sugar and in so doing, converts it into approximately equal quantities of alcohol and carbon dioxide.
Fining – adding a small amount of gelatine to the beer. The gelatine adheres to the suspended yeast and weighs it down, so that it drops out of solution. Adding finings helps produce a clear beer.
Flakes – adjunct grains in precooked, rolled and dried form, which can be added directly to the mash kettle along with the ground malt.
Glucose – a simple sugar directly fermentable by yeast. See *corn sugar*.
Gypsum – calcium sulfate, also sometimes called Plaster of Paris. A water treatment salt which is very useful in brewing "hard water" beers.
Hard water – water containing large quantities of calcium and magnesium salts. See also *chalk*, *gypsum* and *calcium chloride*.
Hops – in brewing, the cones (flowers) of the female hop plant. They contain the bitter resins humulon and lupulon, and other flavoring substances. Hops are boiled with sweet wort to produce bitter wort.
Hop rate – the amount of hops used for a given volume of beer. In commercial brewing, hop rates are quoted in pounds per barrel; amateurs quote hop rates in ounces per five gallons.
Humulon – see *alpha acid*.
Hydrometer – a small glass instrument used to measure specific gravity.
Ion – an electrically charged atom, or group of atoms. Many different ions (such as calcium, magnesium, chloride, sulfate and carbonate) are found in brewing water, where they play a part in the acidity of the mash.

Lactic acid – a mild-flavored acid produced naturally as a by-product of fermentation. Because it occurs naturally in beer, it "blends" perfectly and can be used to control mash pH and neutralize brewing water.
Lager – beer fermented at cool temperatures using a bottom-fermenting yeast, according to traditional Continental practices.
Lauter tub – a vessel with a false bottom and a drain spigot, used for draining the sweet wort off the spent grains and sparging.
Light – can refer to either the color or body of beer. Some light-bodied beers are dark in color, and some light colored beers are full-bodied.
Lupulon – see *beta acid*.
Malt – malted barley grain. This term should *not* be used for malt extract.
Malt extract – commercially made in syrup or powder form; basically it is sweet wort from which all or most of the water has been removed.
Malting – the process of soaking barley in water and letting it sprout, then drying and roasting it in large ovens (kilns) to stop the growth.
Maltose – a simple sugar produced during mashing by the action of beta amylase on dextrins. It is directly fermentable by yeast.
Mashing – the process of steeping (or soaking) ground malt in water, which releases the amylase enzymes from the malt and allows them to convert malt starch to dextrins and maltose.
Maturation – the aging process in which the yeast drops out of the finished beer, and other changes also take place to give beer a smooth, mellow flavor.
Neutralize – to render a chemical solution neutral: neither acid or alkaline. The pH of a neutral solution is 7.0.
Oils – in brewing, various aromatic and flavoring substances contained in the hop cone and extracted during boiling. All hops contain alpha and beta acid; it is the type and amount of oils which give various hop types their distinctive flavors and aromas.
Oxidation – any chemical change caused by and involving oxygen. Beer is oxidised by contact with air.
Pale – a more useful term than light because it clearly refers to color. In England, amber and copper-colored beers are called pale; American use is somewhat different, referring to beers made entirely (or almost entirely) from pale malt.
pH – a measure of acidity or alkalinity. A neutral solution has a pH of seven; higher pH's are alkaline, while lower are acid.
Polyphenol – any of a large group of complex organic compounds found in minute amounts in beer and wine. They are responsible, in part, for chill haze in beer.
Polymerization – the linking together of two or more molecules of like structure to form a larger molecule of different properties. In beer, oxidation of polyphenols causes them to polymerize. The end result is a darkening of the beer and a greater tendency to form chill haze.
Preservative – any chemical which tends to keep beer from oxidation or infection.
Primary – a large plastic trash can in which primary fermentation is carried out.
Primary fermentation – The first, extremely vigorous stage of fermentation, during which the maltose in the wort is changed to alcohol and carbon dioxide.
Primary – adding a small amount of corn sugar at bottling time, in order to bring about a renewed fermentation in the bottle and thus carbonate the beer.

Proteins – an extremely large class of organic compounds made up of carbon, hydrogen, oxygen, and nitrogen. All animal tissue and much plant tissue is made up primarily of proteins. They are responsible for much of the body and head retention of beer, and also for some hazes.
Purity law – see *Reinheitsgebot*.
Racking – siphoning beer from one container to another, leaving the dregs in the bottom of the first.
Reinheitsgebot – literally "pledge of purity" in German; a German law which stipulates that beer be made only from malt, hops, water and yeast.
Resin – a gummy organic substance produced by a plant. Humulon and lupulon are bitter resins produced by the hop flower (or cone).
Salt – usually means table salt, or sodium chloride. However, any compound produced by the reaction of an acid with an alkali is a salt: for example, calcium chloride. Various salts in water can help or ruin the flavor of beer, and promote or decrease the acidity of the mash.
Secondary – any closed container used for secondary fermentation.
Secondary fermentation – the slow stage of fermentation which follows primary fermentation.
Soft water – water containing very small amounts of calcium and magnesium salts.
Sparging – the process of rinsing the spent grains with hot water to retrieve all the sugar from them. It is done after mashing.
Specific gravity – a measure of density. Wort is denser (heavier for the same volume) than water, because of the sugar dissolved in it. The higher the S.G., the more sugar in the wort. See also *Hydrometer*.
Stout – any very dark, robust, full-bodied ale.
Sucrose – cane sugar. Chemically it is a "double sugar" and must be split by the yeast before fermenting. This splitting leaves an acid taste in the finished beer.
Sulfur dioxide – "rotten-egg gas", noxious in excess but useful in small amounts as a preservative in beer and wine.
Sweet wort – the sugar solution produced by mashing and sparging ground malt grains.
Thin – opposite of full-bodied; lacking in body or palate fulness.
Treatment – the addition of a chemical to water in order to alter its characteristics, such as its hardness or pH.
Wort – the liquid solution of malt sugar, before it is fermented into beer. See also *sweet wort* and *bitter wort*.
Yeast – a single celled plant which can ferment sugar into alcohol and carbon dioxide. Pure, pedigreed strains are cultivated by brewers to give the best possible flavor to their beers.
Yeast energizer – a vitamin and mineral supplement used to speed up yeast growth and fermentation.

INDEX

Acetic acid: see *Infections*.
Acid, citric, 42–43.
Acid, lactic, 42–43: see also *Infections*.
Acidity, see *pH*.
Acrospire, 9, 20.
Adjuncts, 10, 21–22, 44–45.
Aging, 11, 12, 66, 100.
Airlock, 13, 61.
Alcohol, 10, 15, 61–62.
Ale, 10, 21, 22, 31–32, 23–24, 81–88.
Alpha Amylase, 46–47.
Anti-oxidant: see *Ascorbic acid*.
Ascorbic acid, 28–29.

Barley, 21: see also *Adjuncts*.
Beta amylase, 46–47, 48.
Bitter (Ale), 81, 83–84.
Bitterness, 10, 26.
Bitter wort, 10, 55–58, 99.
Black patent malt, 20: see also *Roast malt*.
Body, 21, 34, 67, 69.
Boiler, 13, 47–50, 55–57.
Boiling, 9–10, 55–57.
Boilovers, 55.
Bottle brush, 14.
Bottle filler, 14, 64.
Bottle washer, 14, 63.
Bottles, 14, 64, 67.
 labeling, 64.
Bottling, 11, 14, 63–65, 100.
Brewers Calendar, 95–97.
Brown Ale, 81, 84–85.

Calcium sulfate: see *Gypsum*.
Campden tablets, 29, 63.
Capper, bottle, 14.
Carbon dioxide, 10, 15, 63.
Carbonation, 11, 12, 64, 92.
Carboy, 13: see also *Secondary Fermenter*.
Cereal cooker, 36, 44–45, 51–52.
Chalk, 41.

Chlorine Detergent, 14, 63.
Chocolate malt, 20.
Citric Acid: see *acid, citric*.
Cold break, 57, 77.
Cooling, 57, 77.
Corn, 21: see also *Adjuncts*.
Corn sugar, 22, 31, 34, 63–64, 81.
Corona grain mill, 35–36, 39
Crystal malt, 20.
Cubitainer, 13: see also *Secondary Fermenter*.

Dark lagers, 69, 76–79.
Decoction, 38.
Degrees of extract, 58, 92.
Dextrins, 27, 46–47, 48, 50.
Diastase, 10, 40, 46: see also *alpha* and *beta amylase, enzymes*.
Dortmund lager, 75.
Dry hops, 26, 60–61.

Einbeck lager, 78.
Electric stoves, 50.
Enzymes, 9, 40, 46–47.
Extract: see *Degrees of Extract* and *Malt extract*.
Extract beers, 31–34.

Fermentation, 10, 22, 59–62, 81, 99.
Finings: see *Gelatine Finings*.
Finishing hops, 26, 56.
Flakes, 21, 22, 44: see also *Adjuncts*.

Gelatine finings, 28, 61.
Gelatinization, 45.
Glasses, serving, 67.
Glossary, 36, 104–107.
Grain bag, 51–53.
Gravity: see *Specific gravity*.
Grinder: see *Corona grain mill*.
Grinding, 10, 35–36, 39.
Grits: see *Corn*.
Gypsum, 30, 40, 42, 43.

Hard water beers, 40.
Haze, 28–29, 89–90.
Head formation, 69–70.
Heading compound, 30, 64, 92.
Hops, 7, 10, 23–26, 30, 46.
Hop rates, 7, 26, 69, 81.
Hose, racking, 14.
Hot break, 55.
Hydrometer, 15, 57–58, 61–62

Infection, 29, 89.
Iodine test, 93–94.
Ions, 40.
  in brewing water, 40–43.
  adjustment, 43.
Irish moss, 28, 55, 56.

Jugs, glass, 17.

Kilning, 9, 20.

Lactic acid: see *Acid, lactic.*
Lag period, 60, 94.
Lager beer, 8, 12, 33, 69–79.
Lagering, 11.
Lauter tub, 10, 36–37, 51–53.
Light lager, 69–76.
Lime (water treatment), 41.
Line, Dave, 26, 76.

Malt, 7, 9, 10, 19–20.
Malt, British, 9, 81.
Malt, Lager, 7, 9, 28, 46, 69.
Malt Extract, 11, 22, 31.
Malting, 9, 99.
Maltose, 46, 48.
Mash Kettle, 36, 46–50, 51, 55.
Mashing, 7, 8, 10, 38, 46–50, 96.
Mash tun, insulated, 38.
Modification, 9.
Muenchner (Munich lager), 77.

Neutralization, 42–44, 91.
Notebook, 17, 95.

Off tastes, 11, 90–93.
Oils, hop, 10, 26.
Oxidation, 28–29, 89–90.

pH, 43, 46.
PPM (Parts per million), 42.
Pale ale, 69, 81, 82–83.
Pilsner (Pilsen lager), 74.
Pitching, yeast, 10, 60.
Polyclar, 29, 61, 62, 90.
Porter, 81, 86.
Problems, 89–94.
Primary: see *Primary fermenter.*
Primary fermentation, 11, 63.
Primary fermenter, 13, 60.
Priming, 63–64, 92.
Protein, 9, 21, 46, 90.

Racking, 13, 32, 60–67.
Racking tube, 14, 60, 67.
Resins, hop, 10, 23, 56.
Rice, 21: see also *Adjuncts.*
Roast barley: see *Chocolate malt.*
Roast malts, 20–21, 34, 69–70, 81–82.

Scales, 14, 25, 91.
Secondary: see *Secondary fermenter.*
Secondary fermentation, 11, 64.
Secondary fermenter, 13, 64.
Serving beer, 67, 68.
Set mash, 54–55, 93.
Siphoning: see *Racking.*
Skimming, 60, 93.
Soda ash (water treatment), 42.
Sodium chloride: see *Table salt.*
Soft water beers, 40.
Softening water, 42–44.
Sparging, 10, 50–53, 93, 96.
Specific gravity, 14, 16, 57–58, 61–62.
Starch, 9, 10, 46.
Starch conversion, 9, 10, 40, 46, 48, 71:
  see also *Mashing.*
Starter (yeast culture), 28, 56, 59.
Starting gravity, 58.
Sterilizing, 14, 63, 89, 92.
Stout, 21, 81, 87–88.
Strainer, 16, 56.
Sugar, 22, 35, 81: see also *Corn sugar.*
Sulfur dioxide: see *Campden tablets.*
Sweet wort, 9–10, 39, 99.
Sweetness: see *Terminal gravity.*

Table salt, 40, 90.
Taste, 90–93.
Temperature,
   mash, 46–58.
   fermentation, 27, 60.
   storage, 66.
   serving, 67.
Terminal gravity, 47, 57, 61–62, 90.
Test bottles, 30, 64.
Thermometer, 16, 46–47.

Vinegar (acetic acid): see *Infection*.
Vitamin C: see *Ascorbic acid*.

Water, 7, 23, 39–44, 73: see also *pH, Mashing*.
Water softeners, home, 42.
Water treatment, 7, 39–44, 91.
Weight of malt, 39.
Weights & Measures, 103.

Yeast, 5, 27–28, 60, 91.
Yeast energizer, 28.